And There Was Light

An Examination of the Claims of Young Earth Creationist in the Light of the Scriptures and Proven Science

THOMAS C. WEEDON, BSEE, M.DIV.

WESTBOW
PRESS®
A DIVISION OF THOMAS NELSON
& ZONDERVAN

WestBow Press books may be ordered through booksellers or by contacting:

WestBow Press
A Division of Thomas Nelson & Zondervan
1663 Liberty Drive
Bloomington, IN 47403
www.westbowpress.com
1 (866) 928-1240

ISBN: 978-1-9736-2650-3 (sc)
ISBN: 978-1-9736-2651-0 (hc)
ISBN: 978-1-9736-2649-7 (e)

Library of Congress Control Number: 2018904656

Print information available on the last page.

WestBow Press rev. date: 5/3/2018

WHEN GOD BEGAN CREATING THE
HEAVENS AND THE EARTH

(THE EARTH BEING WITHOUT FORM AND EMPTY,
AND DARKNESS WAS UPON THE FACE OF THE
WATERS, AND THE SPIRIT OF GOD WAS HOVERING
OVER THE SURFACE OF THE WATERS),

THEN GOD SAID, "LET THERE BE LIGHT,"

And there was light! *

*This scriptural quote is a translation of the Hebrew text of Genesis 1:1-3 from the Biblia Hebraica Stuttgartensia, 1977 ed. The translation was provided by Thomas C. Weedon

Acknowledgments

Writing a book of this nature can be a very demanding task. I wish to express my gratitude to the following members of my family who supported me in this endeavor by proofreading and correcting the manuscript and counseling me as I strove to produce a book worthy of my readers.

Sylvia J. Weedon, my wife of over 50 years, took time from her busy schedule to read every chapter, providing suggestions to aid and improve readability.

Tamara Mendela, PhD, my daughter, put in many hours to check all my work for grammatical correctness and literary style.

Raymond R. Weedon, nuclear physicist, my brother, proofread my work for correctness in scientific matters.

And thanks to my Lord, Jesus Christ, for His grace that saves for all eternity (John 1:14).

GLORIA DEO

Preface

The differential equations on the front cover of *And There Was Light* were developed by James Clerk Maxwell (1831–1879), a famous Scottish scientist and an elder in the Presbyterian Church of Scotland. Maxwell was noted for his discovery of the classical theory of electromagnetic radiation (EMR). For the first time in history, Maxwell mathematically brought together the phenomena of electricity, magnetism, and light, clearly showing that they were variations of the same thing, what we know also as radio waves. Maxwell's equations proved that the velocity of EMR was always a constant relative to any observer and that it could not be changed.

These phenomena led to Albert Einstein's (1879-1955) quest for an answer to this strange paradox. By 1915, Einstein published his famous paper describing the principles of special and general relativity, based on Maxwell's discovery, and in the early morning of July 16, 1945, in the deserts of Alamogordo, New Mexico, the world was forever changed by the application of Maxwell's equations that resulted in the equation $E = mc^2$.

Today, the Christian world is faced with a new dilemma. We have well-meaning Christians who summarily dismiss any idea in proven science that demonstrates the universe is very old, perhaps 13.76 billion years old. They attack science with an evangelic fervor, seeking to sway the entire Christian world to believe their concept of a recent creation driven by the conclusions of an old Irish bishop, James Ussher (1581–1656). In the seventeenth century, Ussher determined from his Bible studies that God created all that exists in the universe at 9:30 a.m., Sunday, October,

23, 4004 BC. Since the days of Charles Darwin (1809-1882) and his theory of evolution, a war with secularism has existed.

The sad truth is that many leaders of the Christian faith have dismissed all endeavors to show them the actual data and facts that clearly prove a creation billions of years ago. In their book *The Genesis Flood*, Henry M. Morris and John C. Whitcomb claim their principle of knowledge as follows: "We take this revealed framework of history [i.e., the English Bible, 1611] as our basic datum, and then try to see how all the pertinent data can be understood in this context. It is not a scientific decision at all, but a spiritual one."[1]

Simply stated, Morris and Whitcomb believe that all universal facts of the physical universe must agree with their interpretation of the English Bible if these facts are to be believed. That, my dear reader, is called "backward science." In *And There Was Light*, we hold to an inspired Word from our creator God, inspired in the language in which it was first written many centuries ago. And most important, we believe that the God of our Lord Jesus Christ created all that exists, in His time and using His methods. May *And There Was Light* help to shed light on this important subject.

I wish to add an important note at this point. Several times in this book I will make reference to the "English Bible". Please don't misunderstand me. I am merely clarifying an important point and that is the English Bible is not the Bible but is a translation of the Bible. The original Bible was written in an ancient Hebrew language for the Old Testament and in an ancient Greek language for the New Testament. Only the original Bible is inspired of God.

---

[1] Henry M. Morris and J. C. Whitcomb, *The Genesis Flood*, 6th ed. (Grand Rapids, MI: Baker Book House, 1977), xxvi.

Table of Contents

List of Figures

CHAPTER 1

An Introduction

I address *And There Was Light* to all the Bible believers in the world who hold to the creation scenario of Bishop Ussher (1581–1656)—that is, all those who believe in his conclusion that the recent date of the creation of the earth and the universe is taught in the literal understanding of the words in the book of Genesis. In recent decades, a division has intensified among churches over this issue. There are some who believe, with Bishop Ussher, that the creation occurred about six thousand years ago, or to put it more exactly, 9:00 a.m., Sunday, October 23, 4004 BC (according to the proleptic Julian calendar). We can refer to these people as YECs (young earth creationists). Ussher's date of creation has been accepted by many Christians for the last three hundred years. Beginning in 1701 AD, most every edition of the King James Version of the Bible has included Bishop Ussher's chronology in the margins. Perhaps many have assumed that Ussher's chronology is inspired of God as is the rest of Scripture.

However, in our day, there are a growing number of Bible believers who have accepted the overwhelming volume of data and facts that irrefutably demonstrate that the universe, and all that is in it, was created a very, very, very, very long time ago, perhaps going back billions of years. Now, please don't misunderstand my intent. If God had wanted to, He could have created the universe and all that is in it in six seconds, six days, six years, or six million years. However, the evidence shows that God took His time—and He does not owe us an explanation. I plan to shed light on this subject by providing some details that will hopefully be easy to understand and yet that are conclusive with the evidence. So let's begin—let there be light!

Here is the problem as I see it: We live in a world dominated by science. We are taught science from an early age. We experience science every day of our lives, and we have been trained from childhood to think and reason according to rational scientific laws. We need this understanding so that we may function successfully in our modern world, in the job market, in running a household, and in operating the many products of science that we use every day of our lives. Therefore, when we speak to an individual about the things of God or about truths taught in the Bible, we too often have to confront the loud voices crying out that all must believe in a six-thousand-year-old creation because God says so. This ongoing friction causes the inquirer to turn away from scripture and all that it teaches, because he or she knows that it is unacceptable to believe in a six-thousand-year-old creation of the universe and still remain faithful to the common understanding of the world around us. How many souls have been turned away from Christ because they were taught that they must believe in a young earth in order to be true believers? You can't demand that an individual throw out his or her brains just to become a believer in Christ. I personally know some individuals who gave up on believing the Bible because some well-meaning Christians told them that they must believe everything the Bible literally says—principally, in a six-day, 144-hour creation that occurred about six thousand years ago.

There are two very good Christian schools near where I live. In the past, I sent some of my children to these schools. But I recently discovered something very disturbing about these two schools. None of their students go on to study science or engineering after graduation. I believe it is because both of these schools hold, dogmatically, to a young earth theory, and the students have been taught that science is an enemy of Christ, the Bible, and the church. I also know that some graduates from Christian schools who have gone on to a technical or scientific education have dropped away from the church. I believe it is a shame that Christian young people are pushed away from careers in science and engineering. That fact speaks poorly of our faith before a lost and dying world without Christ.

The world knows enough about the creation around them to know that the YECs are to be avoided, and possibly to be pitied. Is it any wonder that many in the world laugh at YECs? As a result, the Bible believer's testimony is discredited or destroyed. Let me summarize by concluding with this claim: Bishop Ussher was wrong. Furthermore, there is not enough evidence given anywhere in the Bible whereby someone could select the date of creation.[1] It just can't be done. In his book *Genesis Unbound*, John Sailhamer states that the dating of the creation week in the Bible leads to erroneous results for two reasons: (1) it assumes that the biblical genealogies are to be understood as strict chronologies, and (2) it assumes that the beginning of creation started on the first day of the week.[2] Neither assumption can be proven to be true. There will be more on this subject in a later chapter.

Hermeneutical principles (the principles of biblical interpretation) have many times been violated when interpreting the first eleven chapters of the book of Genesis. Let me ask the reader this simple question: How can one share the message of God as found in the Bible when he or she must also defend the false teaching of a creation that occurred in 4004 BC? The idea is ludicrous, leading to ridicule and laughter because of the absurdity of the claim. Centuries ago, when the world was not brought up in the knowledge of science (as it is today), a claim of an instant creation might not have sounded so absurd; the population believed in daily miracles and spirit-possessed trees, animals, clouds, and other such things. Moses wrote the first book of the Bible to an audience who knew nothing about the physical nature of the universe. The ancients believed that the earth was flat and fixed (i.e., that it didn't move). Read 1 Samuel 2:8, 1 Chronicles 16:30, and Psalm 93:1 and 104:5 for biblical evidence. If you believe in a literal, word-for-word interpretation of these verses, then you are a "fixed earther."

Today, we know that the earth does move (about sixty-seven thousand miles per hour around the sun). Does this mean that God lied and the Bible has errors in it? No, not if we realize that God was speaking to a very primitive people by our modern scientific standards. He was merely speaking to them according to their intellectual understanding of the heavens and the earth; therefore, the Bible speaks the truth according to the audience for whom it was written.

I believe in the verbal plenary inspiration of the scriptures commonly known as the Holy Bible. This phrase, "verbal plenary inspiration," means that all the words, and every word, of the Bible in the *original language*, as written, are totally ordained by God. The Bible was written to an ancient people of an ancient culture in a setting in which they could understand. I believe that God transmitted the scriptures through His chosen agents, whether they were apostles, prophets, kings, or persons of God-pleasing character. Although errors in the written transmission of the scriptures have occurred throughout the centuries, God's Holy Word has still been preserved better than one part in ten thousand, an accuracy unrivaled by any other piece of ancient literature,[3] and no doctrine of scripture has been lost or compromised.

However, in every case, the scriptures were spoken or written in the common language of the day and in a culture totally foreign to us in the twenty-first century. Let it be added that individuals of the twenty-first century may find it difficult to understand fully the historical, social, political, geographical, scientific, and religious environment of those days in the same way as these things were understood by the people of the Old and New Testaments. When reading the scriptures, it becomes clear that much of what they contain is the history of God's people and their struggles. Over the last several centuries, archeologists have authenticated many of the historical claims of the Bible through their diggings in the Holy Land. Therefore, the Bible has been used on occasion to establish and locate subjects for further archeological research in the Middle East. However, and most importantly, the Bible is a major treatise of the nature and character of the true and only God, the creator of the universe, and we can add that the Bible is actually a collection of historical and theological books written over many centuries to His people.

I believe it is safe to say that the Holy Bible is not, and was never intended to be, a science textbook, despite what some may have considered scientific truth, such as a "flat earth," as was held by the church for millennia based on a common interpretation of scripture. Another example of the Bible being understood as a science text was the church's teaching that the heavens, including the sun, revolved around the earth. This teaching was based on a faulty interpretation of the scriptures. Galileo Galilei (1564-1642) was put under "house arrest" for the last years of his life because he taught that the earth and other planets revolved around the sun. For a time, he faced the sentence of death if he did not stop teaching this so-called heresy. He relented in the face of the threats of excommunication from the church. He didn't like the idea of going to hell, even though he knew that the earth revolved around the sun. Before his death, Galileo wrote a pamphlet outlining the truth of the motion of the heavenly bodies, and this pamphlet was published upon his death.

Let me add this thought: we should never be upset about the Bible not being what it never claimed to be. The Bible does not claim to teach science. Don't go to the Bible seeking scientific axioms. Be satisfied with this simple truth: God created it all, in His time, in His way, according to His purpose, and using His methods, period. Finally, the Bible does not provide an answer to all of humankind's questions. Ask yourself these important questions: Why did God author the first chapters of Genesis? Was it to describe how He made everything, or was it to proclaim that He, the only true God, is the creator of all that exists? The fact that God is the creator of all that exists is my argument for those who suppose God was describing the methods of creation and not the fact of creation.

And the problem continues to this day. I remember attending church as a teen when the pastor declared that humankind would never go into space, based on the clear teaching of the Bible. I heard that sermon on a Sunday morning in the spring of 1957. Four years later, Yuri Gagarin, a Russian cosmonaut, entered space on *Vostok 1*, and orbited the earth on April 12, 1961. The pastor was wrong, but his vitriol against science is still alive and well among many of his parishioners to this day. Because I desired to study science at college, I found his statement a little disconcerting (math and science were my favorite subjects in high school). My grandfather had told me about the time when his preacher had told the congregation that humankind would never fly because the Bible said so, and the Bible doesn't lie. At the time, the Wright brothers had flown their airplane, but they kept the news quiet for several years. When my grandpa discovered the truth, he was troubled about a "god" who would write a book that could be so wrong. I don't know if Grandpa ever overcame his disillusionment with the church, the scriptures, and the preacher. I hope he did.

Sadly, too many Christians are their own worst enemies when it comes to the task of "making disciples" (Matthew 28:19). Do we chase away the seekers by insisting that they must believe in a literal interpretation of

Genesis 1–11 that forces people to disavow the physical truths that they may have learned in school or college and that have been proven beyond repute? Do we jeopardize the future of Christian young people wanting to study science and engineering by insisting that they hold to a six-thousand-year-old universe that was created in 144 hours, in spite of the facts they learn in physics, mathematics, chemistry, geology, astronomy, biology, etc.? Do we insist that they seek to deny to themselves the millions of proven, testable facts of the origin of the universe? Perhaps Augustine (fifth-century church father) was correct when he said, "We do not read in the Gospel that the Lord said, 'I send to you the Paraclete who will teach you about the course of the sun and moon'; for He wanted to make Christians, not mathematicians."[4]

Dr. Stanley Gundry of Moody Bible Institute put it this way in his book entitled *Tensions in Contemporary Theology*: "The doctrine of creation in its basic form simply tells us that God created by an act of His will, in accordance with His purpose. It does not go into detail as to how creation took place; how matter, space and time were spun out of the eternal silence and emptiness."[5]

And herein lies the dilemma. We can't say that we must make a choice between science or the Bible, and when we are faced with evidence of an old earth and universe, we can't throw away our intelligence and believe what we know can't be true. In addition, we can't claim that God made the world to look old just to fool the intellectually elite, as I've heard some pastors and religious educators claim, because God does not lie or deceive (Numbers 23:19; Hebrews 6:18). If the world and the universe were created just six thousand years ago, why then did God leave so much evidence that the creation occurred billions of years ago? What was God's motive in doing this?

Besides, think on this for a moment: if it can be proved that the universe was created in six days (144 hours) six thousand years ago, then every atheist would feel the need to fall on his or her face and repent because the existence of God would have been proven! If you, the reader, would stop and remember the words of scripture, you will recall God's injunction in Hebrews 11:6: "And without faith it is impossible to please Him, for he who comes to God must believe that He is and that He is a rewarder of those who seek Him."

If God provided proof of His existence, there would be no need for faith. So where is the problem? Could it be that we don't know how to correctly interpret various portions of the Bible? As I said before, I believe in a literal verbal interpretation of scripture, and I am a "creationist" (an old earth creationist), but should my interpretation be based on a twenty-first-century AD understanding of the cosmos or on a twentieth-century BC understanding of God's creation? In some cases the literal interpretation just doesn't make sense. Can it be simply because God has not chosen to give the reader enough information to correctly interpret every confusing verse or paragraph, especially where the beginning of everything is involved? Remember, Moses wrote the Torah not to us, but to the people of the Exodus, although it is part of God's revelation to us today.

Proper interpretation of the Bible requires an understanding of the original context in which it was written. This is particularly true for the Old Testament. God chose a specific time, place, and culture in which to inspire faithful persons to produce what we read in the Bible a culture familiar to ancient Mesopotamia and the ancient Near East of the second and first millenniums BC. Understanding their worldview leads to a more faithful understanding of the Bible on our part, and misreading results from assuming the Bible writers thought, believed, and acted as we do today.

This is the paradox that I choose to examine in *And There Was Light*. As one who has received many years of education and practice in science and engineering, as well as having completed many years of education and practice in the Bible and Christian theology, I personally see no conflict between the two endeavors. Others may see a conflict because they see only one side of the issue, the side in which they were trained or are experienced. My answer to all is that God's creation is not yet fully understood by humankind (and may never be).

I believe that behind the intransigence of the YECs is a fear that Charles Darwin's idea of human evolution from the lower species of animals may be correct, if we submit to the claim that the earth is very old, thereby allowing time for evolution. Let me make two observations:

1. Biological evolution is a completely separate idea from the data showing an old earth and universe, and the concept of the modern view of evolution does not automatically follow.

2. Evolution as it is currently understood and being taught has not completed the required tests as demonstrated by the scientific method of inquiry, testing, and prediction; therefore, some in the scientific community are not completely sold on the idea that life began merely by chance, in a swamp millions of years ago, by an accidental mingling of various chemicals, and they have no proof and they cannot replicate the evolutionary process in a laboratory experiment. Therefore they have not succeeded in the scientific method. However, let me make a further observation based on my experience and studies: a slight majority of scientists do believe in a creator God, even if they believe that God used the mechanism of biological evolution to produce modern humankind. I can't say any more about this subject because it is outside of my area of expertise.

If one is a Christian, committed to understanding the scriptures, but also understands the proven facts of geology, cosmology, astronomy, physics, chemistry, biology, and other relevant scientific truths, and if one believes in an old earth, then he or she is called by some a "Christian atheist" or something worse. Name-calling by the young earth creationists is a sad fact of our Christian world today. Tragically, some responsible Christian leaders do little to bring civility to the discussion. I am upset by this prudish, arrogant attitude of the YECs when they refer to, or talk about, well-meaning Christians such as Hugh Ross, C. John Collins, Gleason Archer, Walter Kaiser, John Walton, Francis Schaeffer, and John Lennox—among many others—who hold to a different interpretation of Genesis 1. Yet I have heard lectures by YECs and found their reasoning and scientific facts deplorable and, in some cases, just plain ignorant. And at the same time they call scientists (Christian or otherwise) derogatory names. I presume they believe that they could say just about anything to their Bible-believing audiences and it would be accepted without question (which is true in too many cases). Then, to exacerbate the problem of understanding, I have on occasion supplied the hard geological evidence to a YEC just to have it physically pushed aside so that it could not be seen. This individual did not want to listen to an explanation. I guess he was thinking, *Out of sight, out of mind.*

Christians who follow the teachings of the YECs (with their

pseudoscientific hype, entertaining church lectures about how stupid everyone else is and about the greatness of YECs) are hurting the Christian cause in the United States and making a laughingstock of Christians before the world. I sat in one lecture by a fellow from the Answers in Genesis ministry a few years ago. I caught him in three serious mistakes in just one of his many lectures about basic science, but he had the congregation laughing and applauding in agreement. He spent most of his lecture addressing the teen group, cautioning them not to believe their high school teachers. This is not good witness before an unbelieving world. I have more than a few books written by YEC advocates and I have read them, underlining in red ink the major problems in their arguments. In most cases I have found these YECs serious about their beliefs, but so fixed on a literal twenty-four-hour creation day in Genesis that they have refused to follow the basic principles of hermeneutics, and refused even to look at the billions of pieces of evidence that show a very old universe. For too many Bible believers, the solution is to close their eyes, plug their ears, and turn their heads. How very sad.

It has not always been this way. Many of our famous theologians from the past, even the recent past, accepted an old earth theory and saw that there was no compromise in doing so.

Dr. Benjamin B. Warfield (1851-1921) of Princeton Theological Seminary (1886–1922) writes in his book entitled *Biblical and Theological Studies*, "The Bible does not assign a brief span to human history: this is done only by a particular mode of interpreting the Biblical data, which is found on examination to rest on no solid basis. Science does not demand an inordinate period for the life of human beings on earth: this is done only by a particular school of speculative theorizers."[6]

He continues, "But for the whole space of time before Abraham, we are dependent entirely on inferences drawn from the genealogies recorded in the fifth and eleventh chapters of Genesis. And if the Scriptural genealogies supply no solid basis for chronological inferences, it is clear that we are left without Scriptural data for forming an estimate of the duration of these ages. For aught we know they may have been of immense length"[7]

"The question of the antiquity of man is accordingly a purely scientific one, in which the theologian as such has no concern"[8]

In his book *The Christian View of Man*, John. G. Machen (1881-1937) writes, "It is certainly not necessary to think that the six days spoken of in the first chapter of the Bible are intended to be six days of twenty four hours each. We may think of them rather as very long periods of time."[9]

Westminster Theological Seminary, the seminary that Machen founded, holds the foregoing view even today. In his article "The Early Narratives of Genesis," Professor James Orr, DD (1844-1913), of United Free Church College, Glasgow, Scotland, published in the volumes called *The Fundamentals* (1915) by R. A. Torrey, writes as follows:

> You say there is the "six days" and the question whether those days are meant to be measured by the twenty-four hours of the sun's revolution around the earth—I speak of these things popularly. It is difficult to see how they should be so measured when the sun that is to measure them is not introduced until the fourth day. Do not think that this larger reading of the days is a new speculation. You find Augustine in early times declaring that it is hard or altogether impossible to say of what fashion these days are, and Thomas Aquinas, in the Middle Ages, leaves the matter an open question. To my mind these narratives in Genesis stand out as a marvel, not for its discordance with science, but for its agreement with it.[10]

A classic among Reformed theologians is the work by William G. T. Shedd (1820-1894) where he writes the following: "Respecting the length of the six creative days ... the patristic and mediaeval exegesis makes them to be long periods, not days of twenty-four hours. The later interpretation has prevailed only in the modern church. Augustine teaches that the length of the six days is not to be determined by the length of our week-days."[11]

Following is a portion of a sermon by Pastor Charles Haddon Spurgeon (1834-1892) entitled "The Power of the Holy Ghost," which he preached years before the writings of Darwin were published:

> In the second verse of the first chapter of Genesis we read, "And the earth was without form and void and

darkness was upon the face of the deep. And the spirit
of God moved upon the face of the waters." We know
not how remote the period of the creation of this globe
may be; certainly many millions of years before the time
of Adam. Our planet has passed through various stages
of existence and different kinds of creatures have lived
on its surface, all of which has been fashioned by God.
But before that era came, wherein man should be its
principal tenet and monarch, the creator gave up the
world to confusion. He allowed the inward fires to burst
up from beneath and melt all the solid matter so that all
kinds of substances were cold mingled in one fast mass
of disorder.[12]

In his book *The Greatest Fight in the World,* Spurgeon warns the church
about two sorts of people whom Christians will face throughout this age.
He makes this warning by saying the following:

Two sorts of people have wrought to great mischief and
yet they are neither of them worth being considered as
judges in the matter. They are both of them disqualified.
It is essential that an umpire should know both sides of a
question and neither of these is thus instructed. The first
is the interreligious scientist. What does he know about
religion? What can he know? He is out of court when the
question is; "does science agree with religion?" Obviously
he who would answer this quarry must know both of the
two things in the question. The second is a better man,
but capable of still more mischief. *I mean the unscientific
Christian, who will trouble his head about reconciling the Bible
with science.* He had better leave it alone, and not begin
his tinkering trade. The mistake made by such men has
been that in trying to solve a difficulty, they have either
twisted the Bible, or contorted science. The solution has
soon been seen to be erroneous, and then we hear the cry
that Scripture has been defeated. Not at all; not at all. It is

only a vein gloss upon it which has never been removed.[13]
(emphasis added)

The age of the earth and the age of the universe were not considered much of a problem before Darwin and his infamous lectures and writings *On the Origin of Species*, first published in 1859. But then his idea spread among many schools of higher education, giving pause to those who held the idea of a natural creation with or without God's assistance. This concept aided the growing influence of a form of Christian theology known as theistic evolution, that is, the concept that life was created by God as scripture claims, but the method chosen was to let humankind evolve from the lower species of life via an evolutionary process over millions of years.

In his book *An Outline of Christian Theology*, William N. Clark (1841-1912) (an advocate of the idea of God-directed evolution) writes the following about the creation of the universe and humankind as revealed in scripture: "Accordingly, Christian theology no longer maintains that the earth was created in six days, or that the date to which the genealogies in Genesis lead back, but gives its assent to the antiquity of the planet and the method by which worlds generally have been formed."[14] Dr. William Clark was well-known for his liberal bias or leaning in the interpretation of the scriptures. It is with this statement in his classic work on theology that he opened up a dialogue that continues today within Christian circles, and which is especially refuted by the conservative wing of the Christian church. It is clear that he was trying to accommodate the theories of Darwin and revealed science with the Word of God as recorded in the book of Genesis. In doing so, Dr. Clark was demystifying God's creation and giving credit instead to the natural evolutionary processes that became popular among agnostics and atheists. This led to an outcry among many Christian fundamentalists. Followed shortly by the Bible conference movement that gained in popularity in the early twentieth century, the cry against all who teach an old earth creation reached its pinnacle, and the debate became very bitter and divisive, resulting in the division of the Christian churches.

The purpose of *And There Was Light* is to "let the light shine" on the subject of biblical beginnings and creation, examining first the basic principles of scientific investigation so that the reader may understand why it seems that science ignores God, and second, reviewing the well-known evidence for an old universe, followed by the principles of special and general revelation, principles of biblical interpretation, and then a careful exegesis of the first chapters of Genesis. Christianity is a reasonable faith, not a blind faith. The Lord says, "Come, let us reason together" (Isaiah 1:18).

[1] In the *Zondervan Pictorial Encyclopedia of the Bible*, we read the conclusion, "It is to be observed however that nowhere does the Bible specifically state at what time in the past the universe was created nor what the original state of the heaven and the earth was when made nor how long God was involved in the creative act to activity" (1:989).

[2] John Sailhamer, *Genesis Unbound* (Portland, OR: Dawson Media, 2011), 35.

[3] In most places where errors of transmission (also known as errors in copying or transcription of the text) have been discovered, the cause was limited to simple problems like misspelled words, scribe-added words to aid clarity, or mistakenly omitted words, which, in essence, do not change the meaning of the text. One of the best reference books on this subject is *A General Introduction of the Bible* by Norman L. Geisler and William E. Nix (Chicago: Moody Press, 1986).

[4] *Patrologia Latina*, vol. 42, col. 525, caput x.

[5] Stanley N. Gundry, *Tensions in Contemporary Theology* (Chicago: Moody Press, 1976), 353.

[6] Benjamin B. Warfield. *Biblical and Theological Studies* (Philadelphia: Presbyterian and Reformed Publishing Co., 1968), 239.

[7] Warfield, *Biblical and Theological Studies*, 240.

[8] Warfield, *Biblical and Theological Studies*, 247.

[9] J. Gresham. Machen, *The Christian View of Man* (Edinburgh, Scotland: Banner of Truth, 1984).

[10] James Orr, *The Early Narratives of Genesis*, vol. 6 (Grand Rapids, MI: the Fundamentals, Baker Books, 2003).

[11] William G. T. Shedd, *Dogmatic Theology*, vol. 1 (New York: Scribner and Sons, 1889), 475.

[12] Charles H. Spurgeon, *The Power of the Holy Ghost*, vol. 1, sermon no. 30 (June 17, 1855) (Grand Rapids, MI: Baker Book House, 1990).

[13] Charles H. Spurgeon, *The Greatest Fight in the World* (Dallas: Gideon House Books, 2016), 27.

[14] William N. Clark, *An Outline of Christian Theology* (New York: Scribner's Press, 1894), 222.

CHAPTER 2

Science and the Scientific Method

This chapter is offered to help the reader understand the supposed conflict between science and the Bible. The young earth creationists (YECs) often criticize scientists as if scientists were plotting to destroy religion. In much of the literature published by the YECs, one reads numerous critical and inflammatory remarks about scientists in general. Shamefully, these YECs fail to understand that scientists are people just like them. Some are atheists, some are agnostics, and some believe in a god of some kind or perhaps are deists. It might surprise the YECs to realize that there are actually some scientists who are Bible-believing, churchgoing Christians. But in order to help you understand the scientific mind and the people who think of science as their occupation, we need to examine and understand the attitude of the modern scientist, especially with regard to the literal (word-for-word interpretations) biblical claims of creation.

First I would like to interject this conclusion: the young earth creationists reject the scientific method of determining the actual facts of creation by first assuming that creation occurred in only 144 hours, in 4004 BC, according to the Bible, and then they dream up ideas to try to prove their presuppositions. This is not science, though some would call it "backward science." The YECs have consistently failed to establish even their most basic assumptions, and yet they continue to preach, teach, and publish their assumed facts for consumption by a willing audience of scientifically illiterate Christians, resulting in a public humiliation of the Bible. I contend that there is nothing in the actual facts of the beginning or existence of the universe that contradicts the message of scripture. One can hold to the scientifically proven age of the earth and the age of the universe without compromising his or her faith in God's revealed Word and all that it affirms.

Secondly, I should illustrate the difficulty that exists between scientists and theologians by quoting a passage from a very well-noted seminary professor, Edward J. Young (1907-1968). I have a great deal of respect for this man and his work. He truly is a leading figure in Old Testament scholarship. But with this article quoted below, I have to sadly part company with him and encourage him to contend with the matters for which he was trained. Dr. Young wrote these lines some years ago: "Whenever 'science' and the Bible are in conflict, it is always the Bible that, in one manner or another, must give way. We are not told that 'science' should correct its answers in the light of Scripture. Always it is the other way around."[1]

Dr. Young does not understand the issue of scientific discovery or the experimental method. He assumes that scientists can change their belief systems to fit his interpretation of the biblical account of creation. It doesn't work that way. An honest scientist is bound to believe his or her proven and tested discoveries about our natural universe, not distort them to fit some preconceived notion of the theologians. It is the responsibility of the theologian to check his or her principles of interpretation to determine if he or she has made a mistake. Dr. Young added this final comment in the next paragraph: "The noetic effects of sin lead to anti-theistic presuppositions and inclinations. We must remember that much that is presented as scientific fact is written from a standpoint that is hostile to supernatural Christianity."[2]

As anyone can clearly see, Dr. Young lays the blame for the misunderstanding of Genesis 1 at the feet of science. Now I would be the first to admit that when scientists offer guesses and speculations as answers to earthly phenomena, they may very well be wrong. But when they arrive at their conclusions via the scientific method (i.e., prediction, experiment, and verification through peer review), I have to say that their conclusions are most likely correct. *Scientists cannot change their conclusions concerning proven physical data just to fit someone's interpretation of the English Bible.*

As a bit of background, I find it advantageous to quote from a very interesting book on the subject of faith and science. The conclusion of the authors, Nancy Pearcey and Charles Thaxton, is that modern science owes much to the sixteenth-century Reformation and the liberation of the Bible and Christian beliefs. For you see that it was God, the Creator, who instituted the laws that govern His universe. The laws of nature (or of God, as most theologians believe) demonstrate that the universe is controlled by *knowable* laws (e.g., physics, chemistry, biology, geology, and astronomy), and therefore the universe is knowable, logical, and understandable—not completely, but sufficiently enough to enable humankind to rule over the earth as God had decreed in Genesis 1:28. The following is an excerpt from this book:

> Belief in an orderly universe came to be summed up in the concept of natural law. The phrase "laws of nature" is so familiar to the modern mind that we are generally unaware of its uniqueness. People in pagan cultures who see nature as alive and moved by mysterious forces are not likely to develop the conviction that all natural occurrences are lawful and intelligible. In every culture, of course, craftsmen have developed rough-and-ready rules of procedure. But when they encounter an irregularity or anomaly, they simply accept it as part of the inscrutable nature of things. As historian A. R. Hall points out, the concept of natural law was unknown to both the ancient Western world and the Asian world. When the concept finally arose in the Middle Ages, Hall says, it signified "a notable departure" from anything that had gone before. The source of this departure Hall identified as the Biblical teaching of a Creator. As he puts it, the use of the word *law* in the context of natural events "would have been unintelligible in antiquity, whereas the Hebraic and Christian belief in a deity who was at once Creator and Law giver rendered it valid." The Biblical God is the Divine Legislator who governs nature by decrees set down in the beginning. We see that conviction, for example, in the writings of

17

seventeenth-century mathematician and philosopher
René Descartes, who said the mathematical laws sought
by science were legislated by God in the same manner as
a king ordains in his realm.[3]

A famous quote by Albert Einstein affirms the foregoing conclusion:
"The most incomprehensible thing about the Universe is that it is
comprehensible." An explanation might be that if the universe were
nothing but a collection of random, chaotic things and events, it would
seem very difficult to believe or demonstrate that "it is comprehensible."
Einstein seems to be affirming belief in a divine force behind the
workings of the universe. A significant number of scientists today agree
with Einstein that there must be a creator God. The goal of science (with
a few exceptions) is not to disprove the Bible or the existence of God.
A famous theologian of the nineteenth century, Charles Hodge (1797–
1878), recognized this truth when he wrote in his classic work *Systematic
Theology* the following regarding the Bible and science: "As the Bible is
of God, it is certain that there can be no conflict between the teachings
of the Scriptures and the facts of science. … The Church has been forced
more than once to alter her interpretation of the Bible to accommodate
the discoveries of science. But this has been done without doing any
violence to the Scriptures or in any degree impairing their authority."[4]

I need to add a comment about scientific illiteracy in the United States
today. The problem posed is that some people seem to have a poor grasp
of basic scientific principles and therefore can be easily misled by well-
meaning self-appointed prophets of "homespun" science. The following
report posted on the CNN website seems to support this problem. Sheril
Kirshenbaum from CNN gave this report on February 18, 2014, at 5:09
p.m. EST, entitled "No, the Sun Does Not Revolve Around the Earth."

Every few years, the National Science Foundation
releases its new *Science and Engineering Indicators*, which
feature a barrage of seemingly embarrassing statistics
that detail just how much Americans don't know about
science. The latest such report, out Friday, has caused
a stir by revealing that just 74% of Americans know

the Earth revolves around the sun (conclusion; 26% think that the sun revolves around the Earth). On the surface this figure may seem troubling, but we can take heart: Aside from serving as instant fodder for the news media, quizzing the public tells us little about the state of science literacy in the United States. Science literacy isn't remembering a bunch of facts. It's an appreciation and understanding of the scientific process and the ability to think critically. A lot of smart people get scientific facts wrong, and it doesn't mean they are uneducated. In the 1987 documentary "A Private Universe," Harvard students, faculty and alumni were asked what causes the four seasons. Nearly everyone interviewed *incorrectly* explained that seasons change when the Earth gets closer or farther from the sun in orbit rather than because of the tilt of its axis.

In spite of humankind's fallen condition, God has still given us the ability to understand the physical world we live in. We owe much to science today. Every time you turn around and pick up something in the house, you encounter science. Cell phones, television sets, modern automobiles, and household electronics are just a small inventory of the thousands of items we use daily that are the product of modern science.

For a moment, think of *science* as a verb and not as a noun, because science is what one does, not what one is. Science is not a thing; it is a process. *Science* is the term we use to describe humankind's search for truth/reality in the physical world. Science embraces a procedure, not a conclusion, but science can also refer to the body of knowledge collected over the span of civilization. It is ridiculous to claim science as the enemy of God, even though some scientists may be God's enemy. The endeavor for objective truth about the reality in which we live can always be skewed by presuppositions and prejudice. But these things do not change the truth of reality; they just show that humankind is not fully objective, but instead inbred with an ego that rebels against a supreme being, namely, Almighty God. In this chapter we will examine the basic principles of discovery that are essential to the establishment of fact over opinion.

For most of the last two-thousand-plus years, the intellectual world, more or less, accepted the opinions of the famous Greek thinkers regarding nature, or as we might call it today, science. As an example of some of their opinions and conclusions, the ancients thought that all matter was made up of four things: fire, water, air, and earth. They also believed that the earth was flat. It was fixed and unmovable; it was suspended by giant elephants in a space called the heavens; there was a glass covering (called the firmament, Genesis 1:6–8 KJV) above the earth that contained water that came down through the windows of heaven as rain (Genesis 7:11); and the earth was the center of all creation, with the sun, moon and stars rotating around the earth.

Throughout most of the last twenty-three hundred years, explanations of the workings of the physical universe were based primarily on the teachings and writings of the Greek philosopher Aristotle (384–322 BC). His influence on premodern natural science is immeasurable, mostly in the area of astronomy and cosmology. He arrived at his concepts of natural reality (what we may call "physics") by employing deductive logic and reason. Aristotle was known to have spent hours and days contemplating the workings of the heavens and the unusual phenomena on earth. Therefore, Aristotle believed that reason and logic could solve all scientific problems and present a correct explanation for the way things are. The Greek philosophers loved to debate items of nature among themselves, but the idea of actually performing an experiment to determine who or what was correct apparently never occurred to them.

However, there were several Greek mathematicians who discovered that the earth was actually a sphere when they noticed the different lengths of the sun's shadow at high noon in Egypt as compared to Athens. They performed several experiments to prove their conclusions. But their discovery was ignored and dismissed. With the advent of the Renaissance and thinkers like Galileo Galilei and Sir Isaac Newton, and many others like them, there came to be known a new method of scientific research. Galileo demonstrated this new method, as legend records, when he climbed the Leaning Tower of Pisa and performed the famous experiment of dropping two weights, one heavy and one light. He did this in order to verify the idea that things fall at velocities according to their weight. The popular thought in those days was that heavy objects fell faster than light objects. It occurred to Galileo that perhaps scientific opinion should be proven by experiment. At this time during the Renaissance, many so-called scientists followed Galileo by likewise confirming natural observations of the world through experiment. If these experiments confirmed their observations, then the scientists believed that their conclusions were correct. Again, the proper scientific method came to the rescue of human understanding of nature, God's creation, and showed conclusively that Aristotle was wrong. You can't always arrive at truth in our physical world by opinion, conjecture, logic, or reasoning.

The scientific method is defined by the *American Heritage New Dictionary of Cultural Literacy*, 3rd ed., as "an orderly technique of investigation that is supposed to account for scientific progress." The correct scientific method generally consists of the following steps:

1. careful observations of nature or the phenomenon in question;
2. deduction of natural or physical laws;
3. formation of a theory, or hypotheses and generalizations of those laws for previously unobserved phenomena;
4. experimental and/or observational testing of the validity of the predictions thus made;
5. based on experimental results, making adjustments to the original hypotheses, if required, and repeating the tests until the results sustain the hypotheses or require a new hypothesis; and
6. verification through the process of peer review, where other experts in the field of interest are given an opportunity to investigate the published claims and to prove the conclusions correct or incorrect.

There are occasions when it is not possible for scientists to perform experiments because the subject matter may encompass an abstraction, an idea, or the whole universe. In these cases it is desirable to construct a mathematical model, or a computer model, of the phenomenon and then make predictions to determine if the model correctly predicts the outcome. In this age of the modern high-speed computers, this method is becoming more desirable, since the computer can quickly perform millions of experiments looking for anomalies that would invalidate the original hypothesis. In his book *A Brief History of Time*, Stephen Hawking writes, "A theory is a good theory if it satisfies two requirements. It must accurately describe a large class of observations on the basis of a model that contains only a few arbitrary elements, and it must make *definite predictions* about the results of future observations." Hawking continues, "A scientific theory is just a mathematical model we make to describe our observations."[5]

Only when a scientific inquirer passes all these requirements should the results be classed as true and correct. As we will see in a later chapter about fraudulent science, the conclusions of the YECs fail the scientific method when they come up with ideas designed to fit *their interpretation of the English Bible's description of events involving creation*. As usual, they offer no proof. Instead they try to form ideas to fit their preconceived concept of a literal English Bible understanding of creation, and then offer these ideas as proof of a 144-hour creation that took place in 4004 BC.

The question is, where do scientists come up with these crazy ideas that contradict my Bible? I'm sure some believe that Satan is "alive and well" in every science lab and lecture hall. Now let me state unequivocally that in almost all situations, nothing could be farther from the truth. A working scientist is generally not interested in proving or disproving the Bible. He has a job, and that is to solve problems that incur scientific procedures. That being said, I want to assure the reader that scientists sometimes make mistakes, like everyone else. Sometimes a scientist may cheat or fake the results of a test or experiment just to fit his/ her presuppositions, but in the main, the scientific method is the best method for the impartial study of the unknown. Let's spend some time here looking at the scientific procedures commonly understood as the scientific method.

It's very sad that many of the thinkers in the thousands of years before the Renaissance failed to read their Bibles, because if they had, they would have discovered the scientific method in the book of Daniel. The scientific method can be easily explained as the attempt to prove a hypothesis or a conclusion about nature by performing an experiment. As we now assume, repeated experiments of a particular natural phenomenon are considered proof of the phenomenon when all the experiments produce the same results. In chapter 1 of the book of Daniel, we read of the young

Jewish men who had been taken into captivity by King Nebuchadnezzar of Babylon. These young men were healthy and attractive, and were being placed in the service of the king. Because of this, the steward was ordered to feed these young Jewish men food from the king's table. Daniel rightly observed that some of this food was not according to God's ordinances, and he proposed a different diet plan, according to God's law:

> But Daniel made up his mind that he would not defile himself with the king's choice food or with the wine which he drank; so he sought permission from the commander of the officials that he might not defile himself. Now God granted Daniel favor and compassion in the sight of the commander of the officials, and the commander of the officials said to Daniel, "I am afraid of my lord the king, who has appointed your food and your drink; for why should he see your faces looking more haggard than the youths who are your own age? Then you would make me forfeit my head to the king." But Daniel said to the overseer whom the commander of the officials had appointed over Daniel, Hananiah, Mishael and Azariah, "Please test your servants for ten days, and let us be given some vegetables to eat and water to drink. Then let our appearance be observed in your presence and the appearance of the youths who are eating the king's choice food; and deal with your servants according to what you see." So he listened to them in this matter and tested them for ten days. At the end of ten days their appearance seemed better and they were fatter than all the youths who had been eating the king's choice food. So the overseer continued to withhold their choice food and the wine they were to drink, and kept giving them vegetables. (Daniel 1:8–16)

In this chapter of the Bible, the scientific method is clearly demonstrated. Daniel proved to the king's satisfaction that the dietary principles in the Hebrew Bible were more than satisfactory for a healthy life, and he made this proof by using the method of experimentation. Daniel first made a prediction, and then he conducted a test to verify his prediction. He followed the scientific method correctly. Bright young man, wasn't he?

The problem with Aristotle's scientific method was that it was based on opinions and rational logic concerning observable nature. He never performed any experiments to prove his conjectures or assumptions. He claimed the earth was flat. Did he perform any observations or experiments to demonstrate that the earth was really flat and not spherical? The answer is no. And so it was with most of the ancients' attempts to explain the world of nature surrounding them. The Egyptians, for instance, assumed that most of the bugs that they observed in the swamps had been created by a process of spontaneous generation from the muck and slime in the swamps. No one ever attempted to prove their conclusion.

Now let us look at the difference in the scientific perspectives that we see today. Sir Isaac Newton (1642-1727) is considered to be one of the greatest scientists of the eighteenth century. Newton mathematically described the effects of gravity and the laws of gravity. Once he had codified gravitational attraction as a mathematical solution, he, as well as others, endeavored to prove his conclusions by means of experiment. And thus he is rightly known as a great scientist. In the early nineteenth century, another great scientist, by the name of Michael Faraday (1791-1867), made his mark in modern science when he spent his busy hours performing experiment after experiment concerning the phenomena of electricity and magnetism. These things had been known for many years, but it was Mr. Faraday who performed the thousands of experiments required to document these phenomena in such a way that other scientists could understand and use Faraday's discoveries to develop things like electric motors, high-voltage transmission lines, transformers, and early radio communications. Michael Faraday would always publish the results and conclusions of his experiments in the popular scientific journals of his day so that the scientific community would have an opportunity to examine, test, and critique his findings.

Only in this way can foolish conclusions be refuted and ignored. Without Faraday's experiments, this knowledge would have remained hidden from the world. Born without privilege on a humble estate, without formal education, and personally believing in an almighty creator God and the Bible, Faraday pressed on with his experiments, resulting in many discoveries and much success. In his later years, he was rewarded by being given the chair of Sir Isaac Newton (the highest position) at the Royal Institution of Great Britain, an academy of science. His contributions to the world of electrical science were accomplished though his insistence on using the scientific method throughout his many years of performing experiments.

Faraday brings to mind another genius, an American inventor named Thomas A. Edison (1847–1931). Edison's success was due to his persistent and thorough testing and experiments concerning his many ideas. By using the principles described by the scientific method, Edison was able to invent and produce many electrical wonders that contributed greatly to our American way of life and society in general. And, as we discover, the contributions of famous scientists such as Francis Bacon, René Descartes, Galileo, Newton, Alexander Graham Bell, Benjamin Franklin, Nikola Tesla, and Henry Ford—and thousands of others—are marked by these men's use of the principles of discovery, also known as the scientific method, which requires experimentation.

Perhaps the most upsetting thing about the YECs' arguments is that they attempt to make scientific conclusions about the universe with the purpose of substantiating their presupposition that the universe was created in six twenty-four-hour days, as their interpretation of the English Bible demands. However, they offer no proof. In fact, they struggle just to come up with an acceptable reason for their conclusions, the purpose of which, simply stated, is so that it may fit into their preconceived interpretation of the English Bible. One comment that I have heard and read many times is that since God created Adam and Eve as fully grown adults with the appearance of age, He therefore must have done the same thing with the rest of the universe, creating it with the appearance of age. That idea is mere speculation with no evidence to back it up. The YECs use the scientific method completely backwards. They start with what they want to prove, and then they look for reasons to believe what they want to prove: totally backwards thinking. Using their method, anyone can propose any wild idea they want and then prove it by assuming it is true and finding some loophole solution to satisfy the noninquiring minds.

Some have even said, in all seriousness, that God created everything with the appearance of age just to "fool" the unbelievers or the ungodly. And I say to the YECs: show your proof to the rest of the world, especially the critical scientific world. If your conclusions will stand up to analysis and examination by experts in the fields of study in question, then reveal to the rest of the world that your conclusions are correct. YECs should stand behind their convictions. They should not invent false science in the hope that many others will agree with them in their desire to authenticate the Bible. The Bible does not need their authentication. It can stand on its own very well, like it has already done for thousands of years.

Several years ago, I sat through a lecture by Dr. Albert Mohler, of the Southern Baptist Seminary in Saint Louis, Missouri, where he was speaking on the subject of a six-day creation that took place six thousand years ago. He concluded that God purposely created the universe with the appearance of old age. Concerning the idea that God desires to fool the scientific community, I want to remind all of the following verses:

- "God is not a man, that He should lie, Nor a son of man, that He should repent" (Numbers 23:19).
- "In the hope of eternal life, which God, who cannot lie, promised long ages ago" (Titus 1:2).
- "So that by two unchangeable things in which it is impossible for God to lie" (Hebrews 6:18).

The suggestion that God intended to fool the unbelieving world demonstrates just how weak of an argument the YECs have, that they would even suppose that God could be so dishonest. I have noticed that in the few occasions when I have attended a YEC lecture, the YECs seem to aim their critiques of modern science at the young people. This is very sad, as it poisons the minds of the young, leading them to distrust science and perhaps not attempt a science or engineering career. The United States needs scientists and engineers for our future as a nation. I personally would like to see more Christian scientists and engineers. We are already falling behind the other nations of the world.

In the conclusion of this chapter, I need to address the philosophy of scientism. As a result of the growth in the number of "freethinkers" from the beginnings of the Renaissance, a new philosophy arose that took the principles of science and the scientific method and adapted them to the search for wisdom and knowledge, especially the knowledge of the unknown, such as God, life after death, the meaning of life, and the existence of spirits. The following statement is true based on the philosophies of scientism: *Truth must be limited to the information accumulated by the five senses of humankind.* Since no person can see, feel, taste, hear, or smell God or the angels, or heaven or the spirit world, then according to the principles of scientism, none of these things exist. Modern scientists have invented tools that embellish the five senses of humankind, making it possible to detect the reality of the very small (molecules and atoms) and the very large (galaxies), but these tools do not and cannot tell us about the reality of God.

Therefore, according to the philosophy of scientism, these unseen things like gods and spirits cannot and do not exist. Of course, this philosophy is false and misleading, because it does not account for the fact that humankind's five senses may be limited and are not able to reveal to human beings the true nature of creation and reality. I believe that the modern realm of quantum physics has shown us that there is more to reality than some are willing to admit (an invisible realm). Sadly, however, scientism is being readily adopted by our modern educational facilities, and these ideas are affecting the minds of our youth. Because of scientism, the Christian faith is being attacked on all fronts and Christianity is becoming more unpopular every day. May I suggest that the faithful should not engage in promoting ideas that are not true? We need to stay focused on the truths of scripture.

I want to add a special note to the end of this chapter, and that is the concept of biological evolution. This popular idea cannot be verified using the scientific method of experiment and observation. So the idea that humankind accidently evolved from a lower species of animal is, at best, an educated guess or speculation. Likewise, the concept that life began as an accidental collection and mingling of various chemical compounds requires a greater faith than does belief in a supernatural Creator. Every biological scientist knows that you can collect all the elements found in a living cell, and every biological scientist knows that there is no way one can make the collection of elements morph into a living, multiplying, self-replicating cell. You may question the motives of the ardent evolutionists by suggesting that they presume to destroy the credibility of the Bible, and in this you may be correct. I'll leave that option open for the reader of *And There Was Light*.

In the next chapter we will examine the question of natural revelation: is it believable or not?

---

[1] Edward J. Young, *Studies in Genesis One* (Nutley, NJ: Presbyterian and Reformed Publishing Co., 1976), 53.

[2] Young, *Studies in Genesis One,* 53.

[3] Nancy Pearcey and Charles Thaxton, *The Soul of Science: Christian Faith and Natural Philosophy* (Wheaton, IL: Crossway Books, 1994), 26.

[4] Charles Hodge, *Systematic Theology*, vol. 1 (Grand Rapids, MI: Eerdmans, 1979), 573

[5] Stephen Hawking, *A Brief History of Time* (New York: Bantam Books, 2001), 15, 179.

CHAPTER 3

General Revelation vs. Special Revelation

A good definition of *divine revelation* from a historic point of view is given as follows: "Revelation is God's disclosure of Himself through creation, history, the conscience of man, and Scripture."[1]

There are two principal revelations from God, as follows:

1. the Word of God, the Bible (special revelation), and
2. the works of God, the universe and all that is in it (general or natural revelation).

Special revelation is the revelation that comes directly from God, and we accept the Bible as the sum total of His revelation to us today. We must accept the Bible, by faith, as that special revelation. Now we must acknowledge that God's revelation to us is progressive. He didn't give all of His revelation in Genesis. God progressively added His revelation over the entire duration of the lives of the prophets and apostles as they wrote Holy Scripture. Therefore, we should not assume that Genesis tells us everything we need or want to know about creation. There are many more passages in scripture that add to this subject, and before we rush to some conclusion, we must study them all. But always remember this truth: since God cannot lie or deceive, the words of the Bible and the facts of nature must agree.

It is important to note that there can be no conflict between these two revelations, because if there is, then one must surmise that God is schizophrenic or that our understanding of the physical world is flawed.

We'll address this subject in a later chapter. However, general revelation *does not* teach us the way of salvation, but it does teach us that there must be a creator and that this creator is all-powerful. "The heavens are telling of the glory of God; And their expanse is declaring the work of His hands" (Psalm 19:1).

General revelation also teaches us that God is good in His basic character, as all of His creation fits our definition as being good, that is, good for life and good for humankind. "And yet He did not leave Himself without witness, in that He did good and gave you rains from heaven and fruitful seasons, satisfying your hearts with food and gladness" (Acts 14:17).

Paul listed general revelation as adequate to teach humankind an important principle: "For since the creation of the world His invisible attributes, His eternal power and divine nature, have been clearly seen, being understood through what has been made, so that they are without excuse" (Romans 1:20).

"What we claim as Christians is that, when all of the facts are taken into consideration, the Bible gives us true knowledge, although not exhaustive knowledge."[2] What is meant by general revelation is that which is given to all human beings, in nature and history, and in the nature of humankind itself. The reality and validity of revelation in this sense is declared in scripture verses such as Isaiah 40:26, Exodus 9:16, Acts 14:15–17, and Matthew 6:26. Paul clearly mentions this truth in his epistle to the Romans: "For when Gentiles who do not have the Law do instinctively the things of the Law, these, not having the Law, are a law to themselves, in that they show the work of the Law written in their hearts, their conscience bearing witness and their thoughts alternately accusing or else defending them, on the day when, according to my gospel, God will judge the secrets of men through Christ Jesus" (Romans 2:14–16).

General revelation is on a par with special revelation, limited by humankind's interpretation and understanding. We are told in the Bible that the natural man cannot receive (understand) the things of God (2 Corinthians 4:3,4); therefore, general revelation cannot always penetrate the spiritual blindness of the natural man. But this verse does not imply that general revelation is not true or not worthy of belief. Through general revelation, humankind can know a limited amount of truth about the natural world and the universe. Truth discovered in the natural world is just as true as spiritual revelation, because it is from the same God.

It is very interesting to find that the famed scientist and noted atheist Stephen Hawking should write in his book *A Brief History of Time* the following comment: "It would be very difficult to explain why the universe should have begun in just this way, except as an act of God who intended to create beings like us."[3] So we see that even general revelation can lead some of the most intelligent people in the world to an acknowledgement of a Creator, even though they don't want to believe in a supreme Creator and a savior God.

The Bible is revealed truth from God, but so is creation (nature, the world, the universe, physical creation), because it also is from the same God. Therefore there must be harmony between both revelations. If discoveries of natural phenomena contradict the revealed Word of God, then there can only be one of two reasons. Either our interpretation of the scriptures is incorrect or our understanding of the natural phenomena is incorrect. I can't think of another alternative. The issue of natural or general revelation was addressed many years ago in the Belgic Confession, AD 1561, Article 2, "The Means by which We Know God," which begins as follows:

> We know him by two means: First, by the creation, preservation, and government of the universe, since that universe is before our eyes like a beautiful book in which all creatures, great and small, are as letters to make us ponder the invisible things of God: his eternal power and his divinity, as the apostle Paul says in Romans 1:20. All these things are enough to convict men and to leave them without excuse. Second, he makes himself known to us more openly by his holy and divine Word, as much as we need in this life, for his glory and for the salvation of his own.

When God created the universe, He created it with physical rules or laws. Examples are the law of gravity, the law of electrodynamics, Newton's laws of motion, quantum physics, and special relativity. And there are thousands of other laws regarding the fields of physics, mathematics, chemistry, biology, astronomy, geology, etc. Humankind did not create these laws. We discovered them! God created these laws when He created the universe and made order out of chaos ("the earth was formless and void" [Genesis 1:2]). It is these laws that allow humankind to understand the world and the universe that we live in. Without these laws, all creation would be a confusing mess and human beings could not survive in a world that they could not comprehend. How could human beings make themselves tools, build houses and cities, sow and harvest crops, build transportation systems and communication systems, and so forth?

For a lack of a better term, let us call these rules or laws that God instituted for His creation "scientific laws." Since the time of creation, humankind has struggled to learn these scientific rules in order to build themselves a better world. Natural or general revelation tells us that when we hit our finger with a hammer, it will hurt. We also learn through natural revelation that the circumference of a circle is equal to 3.1415926 … times the diameter of a circle. Natural or general revelation tells us that the hypotenuse of a right triangle is equal to the square root of the sum of the squares of the opposite sides of the triangle. Natural revelation has shown us that all matter is made up of miniature particles that we call atoms, and these particles obey natural laws which humankind has discovered in our quest to build the physical society that we have today. It is these physical laws that humankind has discovered in our endeavor to understand the universe that God has created. We choose to call this endeavor "science." Our cell phones and iPads are some of the popular results of this scientific knowledge.

Therefore when we read someone's interpretation of scripture that violates one or more of these physical rules or laws of nature, we are left with only a few possibilities or conclusions, as follows:

1. that the person misunderstood or misinterpreted scripture, or
2. that God momentarily changed or modified the physical laws of His creation, or
3. that there are still some physical laws of creation which we do not understand.

Item 3, the last conclusion, closely borders on the concept of miracles, which may be a possibility to consider. The second conclusion is the one most often used by the YECs when they attempt to explain why the created things of this world appear the way they do, such as why the light from distant stars, a million light years away, appears, when they claim that only six thousand years have passed since God created everything. Let me remind the reader of this valuable truth: God has no intention to deceive humankind. Therefore, if He chose to alter the physical laws of the universe just to make it appear that He created everything on 9:30 a.m., Sunday, October 23, 4004 BC, then we would have a case against God and His promise never to lie or deceive. Please refer to my comments in chapter 2 concerning God's promise. In conclusion, we are left with only one possibility, and that is conclusion no.1: someone has failed to understand and interpret the scriptures correctly. May I suggest those who preach a young earth?

The Bible clearly illustrates the advantages of general revelation in many verses. For instance, we are shown the benefit of honest labor when we read Proverbs 6:6: "Go to the ant, O sluggard, Observe her ways and be wise." Proverbs 30:18–31 mentions ants, eagles, badgers, locusts, lizards, lions, and roosters, using all these insects and animals as examples for our education in human behavior. God tells Job (in Job 38–39) to look at the stars, the heavens, and all creation as an example of God's power and knowledge. As the psalmist writes, "Great are the works of the Lord; They are studied by all who delight in them" (Psalm 111:2). The psalmist says that it is good to study the works of God! So even God says we need scientists and engineers.

The study of God's creation, that is, general revelation, is profitable for all. Paul explained that all creation is a witness to the living God in Acts 14:15–17, as follows:

> Turn from these vain things to a living God, Who made the heaven and the earth and the sea and all that is in them. In the generations gone by He permitted all the nations to go their own ways; and yet He did not leave Himself without witness, in that He did good and gave

you rains from heaven and fruitful seasons, satisfying
your hearts with food and gladness.

God did not leave Himself without a witness. Thus the scriptures are full of examples proclaiming that God's creation is a testimony to His power and glory, but the heavens teach us little about God's attributes and purposes. God called His creation "good" not because of any moral attributes of His creation, but because His creation satisfied His purpose, which was to serve as an appropriate place for humankind to live.

May it be confirmed one more time: General revelation is just as important to humankind's well-being on earth as special revelation is for humankind's well-being in God's coming kingdom. General revelation can teach humankind all we may need to know to survive on earth and to create peaceful civilizations, modern conveniences, and a good life. All the scientific laws of our physical universe that humankind has discovered are part of God's creation and are also part of His general revelation to humankind. So when I hear someone claim that God's special revelation is more important than His general revelation, I immediately expect an attack on science and all that it stands for. Special revelation and general revelation are two different things and they must not be confused. The Bible is special revelation, because it teaches us about God, His attributes, and His purposes for humankind. These things one cannot know by observing nature or, as we may say, by general revelation.

[1] M. C. Tenney, ed., *The Zondervan Pictorial Encyclopedia of the Bible*, vol. 5 (Grand Rapids, MI: Zondervan, 1975), 86.
[2] Francis A. Schaeffer, *Genesis in Space and Time* (Downers Grove, IL: Intervarsity Press, 1975), 35.
[3] Stephen Hawking, *A Brief History of Time* (New York: Bantam Books, 2001), 163.

CHAPTER 4

Principles of Biblical Interpretation

In this chapter, I wish to explain why it is important to understand the proper way of interpreting the written word while seeking an understanding of the biblical text discussing God's creation, be it young or old, or sudden or gradual, and His purpose and methods of creation. After reading this chapter, ask yourself, do the young earth creationists (YECs) follow correct principles of biblical interpretation?

It has been said that the cause for the many different denominations within the Christian church is improper hermeneutics. Hermeneutics is the study and application of the principles of literary interpretation. It seems that Christians throughout the centuries have had a continuing problem with biblical interpretation. So for every argument over a point in scripture, a new denomination was formed. I'm not sure if this statement is true or not, but it bears some consideration. To further illustrate the concept of biblical interpretation, I believe the following statement from a popular textbook on hermeneutics best explains the underlying principle: "Simply stated, the task of interpreters of the Bible is to find out the meaning of a statement for the author and for the first hearers or readers, and thereupon to translate that meaning to modern readers."[1]

When you read scripture, what comes across to your mind? Are you looking at it as if you were reading a personal letter to you or to your neighbors in today's world? Or are you looking at and reading scripture as if it is a recording of God's words and actions to an ancient people thousands of years ago? How did ancient human beings living three thousand to eight thousand years ago understand the world around them? Thomas Africa, the author of the book *The Ancient World*, wrote these words describing the thought process of the ancients: "Early man assumed that the material world was alive as he was and he filled it with spirits; trees, streams, fire, even rocks and all were made alive and had personalities and terrible things like storms or volcanos were powerful beings to be feared and placated."[2]

So the question remains, how did ancient human beings view the world? The answer is that the ancients saw the world and the universe completely different from the way we see it today. It is totally wrong for us to assume that we can understand a letter written to the ancients in the same way that we would comprehend a letter written to us today. Keep this principle in mind as you study the ancient books of the Bible. Further, we must avoid the extreme of mystical pietism, which is demonstrated by those who teach or believe that the Holy Spirit specially teaches them the true meaning of a passage of scripture as they read it. Instead, try to understand the text as it was meant by the original author to be understood.

When Moses wrote the first five books of the Bible, was he writing with the purpose in mind to teach you and me about the laws of God, the ways of God, and the thoughts of God, or was he writing to his fellow Hebrew people who had just been liberated from the terrible ordeal of slavery in Egypt? I believe that when we read the ancient words of Moses, we are actually reading an ancient letter to an ancient people. It has been said that when we read the scriptures, we are really reading someone else's mail. Of course, scripture was written for our benefit, and for the benefit of all believers throughout the ages, as it teaches us the truth about God and the way of salvation, but remember this simple axiom: scripture was not written *to* us, but *for* us. Next, also remember this truth: the Bible contains a prescientific worldview, and it also contains a supernatural worldview in much of its teaching. Therefore, in some places, it may very well be useless to interpret the Bible using a twenty-first-century construct.

Could it be that Moses was being led by the Holy Spirit to write to the Hebrew people who had been prisoners of the Egyptians for four hundred years, writing in their language and according to their cultural understanding? Would it not make sense to conclude that Moses was writing the words as led by God to teach the Hebrew children about the one true supreme God?

> "But know this first of all, that no prophecy of Scripture is a matter of one's own interpretation, for no prophecy was ever made by an act of human will, but men moved by the Holy Spirit spoke from God" (2 Peter 1:20–21).

Remember that the Hebrew people, the descendants of Abraham, were essentially raised for four hundred years in a pagan culture as slaves, where they knew little or nothing about the God of Abraham, Isaac, and Jacob. They needed this basic teaching as the foundation of a new nation of Israel, which God was going to create for them (not for us). Therefore, it makes sense that Moses was not writing to the Hebrew slaves about things related to the science of his day. In that day, everyone knew that the earth was flat and was suspended on the backs of giant elephants or mountains, and that the sky was a solid bronze dome that covered the earth. Moses was not writing either to support or deny this popular belief. Moses was being led by God through the Holy Spirit to write down the history of the descendants of Abraham, beginning, of course, at the very beginning, that is, of the world and the heavens as these people understood such things. This is important to understand, because when we read about ancient cultures, we discover that most all of the heathen nations believed in numerous gods, and nations generally believed that none of their gods created the universe but had been created by other gods, and then the lesser gods created humankind to be their servants. So after a general review of the pagan religions of the ancient world, it becomes very obvious that Almighty God, the God of Abraham, Isaac, and Jacob, needed to teach the children of Israel about the real and true God. God's revelation to Israel had to be culturally decipherable. Keep this idea in mind as you read the first five books of Moses.

God did not use Moses as a typewriter. Moses was writing to his people in his language, according to his cultural opinions, according to the Hebrews' understanding of the existing world, and also according to their traditions and their intellectual abilities. It is obvious that after four hundred years of captivity, imprisonment, and slavery, the descendants of Abraham, the Hebrew children held captive in Egypt, had a very poor understanding of the physical world around them and an extremely poor understanding of the omnipotent creator God.

Therefore I wish to conclude that the purpose for which God was using Moses in writing the Pentateuch was essentially to teach the Hebrew children the truth about the only God, the Creator God, the true God of the universe, the God whom they were called to worship and to serve, and to rid their mind and understanding of the false gods of the pagan lands in which they'd served for so long. And when Moses wrote to his people, he wrote in a language and according to a cultural viewpoint that they could understand. Moses did not mention that the earth was a sphere, or that it revolved around the sun, or that the earth was part of a solar system that was part of a giant galaxy known as the Milky Way, composed of billions of stars, and surrounded by billions of galaxies, each containing billions of stars. If Moses had said these things to the Hebrew people, they would have laughed at him and would have believed that he was crazy or possessed by demons. Do you see the problem? Moses's writings definitely do not include any reference to modern science.

We cannot impose a modern scientific worldview or understanding of the universe onto the literature of the Bible. In fact, the Hebrew language had no word for "universe." To the ancient Hebrew, the idea of the universe was contained in their simple phrase "heavens and earth." The word *heavens* referred to the sky above and the domain of God. The word *earth* referred to that visible land which surrounded them, as well as to the dirt under their feet. When the Bible mentions the "circle of the earth" (Isaiah 40:22 ESV, KJV, NIV), it is referring to the circle that the inhabitants saw when they looked at the horizon that surrounded them. In no way did the ancient Hebrew ever conceive of a planet called Earth, shaped like a ball, orbiting 93,000,000 miles from the sun, and suspended by nothing in a vast and empty universe, as we understand it today.

So when Moses began writing the Torah (the first five books of the Bible, also known as the Pentateuch), God directed him to make it very clear that everything that exists was created by the God of Abraham (John adds to this in his gospel—John 1:3). Now Moses could not write about the method or procedure by which God created everything, because no one would understand. Furthermore, Moses could not tell the people that God took thousands or millions or billions of years to create everything, again because no one would understand. Let me make this point very clear: Moses had to write so that the people would understand the Creator, not the created. "The doctrine of creation in its basic form simply tells us that God created by an act of His will, in accordance with His purpose. It does not go into detail as to how creation took place: how matter, space, and time were spun out of the eternal silence and emptiness."[3]

It is important to remember this basic principle concerning God's purpose for the book of Genesis: God needed to teach His people that the gods of Egypt were not real, but fictitious and imaginary, and the invisible realm of Satan was the power behind these false gods. Viewed with respect to its negatives, Genesis 1:1–23 is a polemic against the mythico-religious concepts of the ancient Orient.[4]

We accept the concept of biblical inerrancy by faith. This inerrancy truly reflects the ideas of God, sin, and salvation, but does not necessarily extol the facts of science and the physical universe. The Bible was not written with the purpose of teaching the reader about the physics of the natural world, or biology, or geology, or chemistry, but instead it was written with the purpose of teaching us about the true God and humankind's relation to Him. In the Bible, the ancient views of the physical universe were *accommodated* for the sake of the original readers.

Biblical interpretation has always been a source of conflict and misunderstanding, perhaps no more so than with scientists or those who study the physics of the natural world. This is best illustrated by an account of the thoughts of a great scientist and Christian man, James Clerk Maxwell (1831–1879), of Edinburgh, Scotland. Like Faraday and like Newton, Maxwell believed that God made the universe, that the laws of physics were God's laws, and that every discovery was a further revelation of God's great design. At the same time, as a devout Christian, he believed that the true nature of God was to be found in the Holy Bible, which he knew as well as any scholar of divinity. In his scientific work he treated all theories, including his own, as provisional, until they had been backed by experimental results. How was this approach to be reconciled with a Christian faith that required absolute trust and belief in the absence of material evidence? Much of the answer lay in how the scriptures were *interpreted*. This process of interpretation wasn't easy, but for Maxwell it was necessary. He couldn't keep his science and religion in separate compartments.[5]

James Maxwell was famous for his development of the mathematical laws of electromagnetic radiation (the form of light rays, radio rays, cosmic rays, etc.), but he was also a devout Christian. He was an elder in the Presbyterian Church of Scotland, and as was his custom, following dinner every evening, he held Bible study and prayer time for all who were in his house. Since he was a scientist by training, you can understand that at times Maxwell had problems with a literal interpretation of some passages in the Bible. However, that did not stop him from worshipping his God, Jesus Christ, who bought his salvation.

So the issue is simply a matter of interpretation. When we see a conflict between the facts of God's creation and God's Word, we have a problem either in our interpretation of the facts of the physical world or with our interpretation of His Word. Therefore let us review the principles of biblical interpretation to ensure that we know of what we speak.

1. All biblical interpretation must be based on the original written text of scripture, not the English text or any other translation, but the text that the prophets of old used when writing. For the Old Testament, that would be Hebrew and Aramaic. Of course, preliminary studies can be most successful by using a more modern, literal English translation. That means one should try to first avoid a paraphrase version, or a periphrastic English translation. Use several literal English translations and compare your findings, and then add a good and trusted periphrastic version to your reading. That way you should be satisfied that your understanding is the best possible. Also, if you don't know the original language, you may want to read some source material written by experts in the original language.

2. All biblical interpretation must be established based on the understanding of the original readers or hearers. You must understand the readers' culture, their concept of history, and their understanding of nature and the world around them before

you can draw any more conclusions as to meaning of the text. It is important to remember this simple truth: Moses wrote what God was leading him to write, and his texts were written to the huge Hebrew crowd whom he had led out of the pagan world of ancient Egypt. You have to ask yourself the question about *purpose*. When God led Moses to write Genesis, you need to ask why. What was God's purpose? Was it to teach the ancient Hebrews about the science of the universe? Now, for a moment, think on this idea: what do you think the ancient Hebrews knew about the world around them? If you want to know what they thought, please refer to some of the books on ancient cultures listed in the bibliography. You will be amazingly surprised.

A serious problem exists among the clergy today, because too many fail to explain the historic and cultural meaning behind the texts that they may be teaching. Here is a comment by a renowned Old Testament scholar, Dr. Walter Kaiser: "The Achilles heel for many among the trained clergy is the failure to bring the Biblical text from its B.C. context and to relate it directly and legitimately to the present day."[6]

Let me add a paragraph to illustrate the importance of communicating on the level of your intended audience (as the Hebrew was far below our understanding of the world and the universe). I remember as a young fellow that I would ask my mother some serious questions about life. One question I asked her is, "Where do babies come from?" I don't remember how old I was when I first asked this question, but Mother would always answer, "The stork brings them." In time I began to think that she was telling me a lie, just like when she told us children about the Easter Bunny and Santa Claus. Then came the day when I was about twelve years old. Mom finally broke down and told me the truth about "the birds and the bees." I must admit that I was depressed for some time after, but the truth is always better than an innocent lie. My mother felt that she had to wait for me to gain a certain level of maturity before she could tell me about some of the hard facts of life. Simply stated, Mom had to *accommodate my immaturity*. I believe that God had to accommodate the ancient

Hebrews' immaturity concerning matters of advanced physics and astronomy. I trust that this example can help you understand the importance of culture and mental maturity in personal communications.

3. All biblical interpretation should be undertaken with a generous measure of common sense. What do I mean by this? Simply put, God gave us brains, and He expects us to use them. As an example, let me mention that the apostle Paul would not be qualified to be an elder or deacon of a church, because he said to his student Timothy that an elder or deacon must be the husband of one wife. Paul had no wife. He was single, so based on a literal interpretation of the Bible, he is disqualified for the offices of elder and deacon. Does that make sense? In fact, the Bible does not mention if the restriction applies to only one wife for all time or one wife at a time. Do you see the problem? In biblical interpretation, we must apply some level of common sense.

Yes, I know that the Bible, our theology, teaches us that the unregenerate human being is darkened in understanding. But everyone has some measure of what we call common sense. By this statement, I do not wish to discount miracles. Supernatural events, or miracles as we sometimes call them, could be another aspect of our existence that we do not know enough about in order to form an understanding. Science has not, nor may it ever, unfold all there is to know about our physical universe. God created it with many mysteries yet to be understood or discovered. But one thing is clear: God made the universe in accordance with His laws that preserve order (not chaos), and I don't believe God violates His laws in a way that would bring disorder. Instead God may supersede His laws with a higher law in order to bring about His desired results. But we cannot cite a miracle when the physical evidence proves otherwise.

4. The Bible must be interpreted according to its genre. As an example, certain books and passages in scripture were written as a historical record for the Hebrew people, particularly, Joshua

through to Esther. Other books were written for the purpose of worship, such as the Psalms. Some were written for the purpose of instruction in wisdom, such as Proverbs and Job. The Prophets were written as warnings to the people of Israel—warning of God's coming judgment because of their sins. So it can be easily demonstrated that attempts at interpretation must include the Sitz im Leben, the "life setting" of each book, thereby making correct interpretation possible. This idea is further understood by the newly derived concept of discourse analysis, which is a tool developed to aide in understanding the message of the written text. It should be obvious to all serious readers of Genesis 1–11 that the material is very different from most of the rest of the Old Testament.

5. The Bible must be interpreted according to the history, manners, and customs of the ancient world. A study of history gives us the background of an event recorded in the Bible. If we fail to study history, we do so at our own risk and may very well arrive at a wrong conclusion in our understanding. The manners and customs of the ancient world help us to understand the mental and emotional climate of the ancient world. We also need to study the various religions of the ancient Near East so that we can understand the thinking of the Hebrew people in the ancient land of Canaan. Our study of history should also include a study of archeology, geography, and topography in the historical context of the Middle East. Failure to include these things may also lead us to wrong conclusions. Dr. Michael Heiser wrote, "The proper context for interpreting the Bible is the context of the biblical writers."[7]

6. Biblical passages should be interpreted according to the type of speech observed. That is, does the speech or writings include various types of literary forms, such as poetry, prose, and narrative, or is it based in wisdom or of an apocalyptic nature? An exegete must also look for various forms of speech, like tense, mood, and aspect, in the text. Furthermore, care must be taken

to observe repetitions, parallelism, parables, hyperbole, and various types of figures of speech such as similes and metaphors. Finally, in interpretation, context is always king according to my seminary professors. Always be certain that your interpretation clearly fits the intent and context of the passage, paragraph, chapter, and book that is being studied.

7. Let me add this last section discussing that I believe is very important to understand. God knew that the earth is a sphere of eight thousand miles in diameter, held in space by the gravitational pull of the sun, 93 million miles away, so why didn't He explain this fact instead of letting the Hebrew tribes believe something otherwise that was not true? Did God say that He does not deceive?

   • "God is not a man, that He should lie, Nor a son of man, that He should repent; Has He said, and will He not do it? Or has He spoken, and will He not make it good?" (Numbers 23:19).
   • "Also the Glory of Israel will not lie or change His mind; for He is not a man that He should change His mind" (1 Samuel 15:29–30).
   • "His grave was assigned with wicked men, Yet He was with a rich man in His death, Because He had done no violence, Nor was there any deceit in His mouth" (Isaiah 53:9).
   • "In order that by two unchangeable things, in which it is impossible for God to lie" (Hebrews 6:18a).

If these assertions are true, then why did God not explain to the people of Israel that the heavens are not layered as they may have thought, but that the heavens above their heads are simply a shell of invisible gas, mostly nitrogen and oxygen, extending far above their heads for many miles and then fading into an empty region called space, where the moon and stars and distant galaxies dwell, and that the sun and all the heavenly hosts look like they are circling the earth because the earth rotates once every twenty-four hours? Why was the apostle Paul misled to mention that he was taken up into the third heaven (2 Corinthians 12:2–4), when there is no third heaven above earth? Do you see the problem? Did God accommodate His revelation to Moses and the children of Israel to fit into their realm of understanding? Could God have explained His process of creation (Genesis 1–2) any other way and still have the Hebrew people understand? I don't believe He could. God had to reveal Himself to Moses and the people in a frame of reference that they all could understand and still believe in the one true God, the only God, the Creator of all things great and small, human and beast, mountain and valley, heaven and earth. When we, as occupants of the twenty-first century, read the Bible, we must always remember this fact: it was written to the Hebrews in the wilderness, not to us. In effect, we are reading someone else's mail.

I believe that the principles of biblical interpretation have been adequately covered in this chapter. For those interested in further study, look to the bibliography for more recommended reading material. On the popular level, I recommend a book by Dr. Gordon Fee,[8] and for a more serious study, the book by Walter Kaiser and Moisés Silva.[9] Don't accept any recommendations that suggest you read and understand the Bible in the common language and cultural setting of the twenty-first century only. That was never intended by God.

Next, in chapter 5, we will survey some examples of improper hermeneutics that we find written in some of the popular young earth creationists' literature in today's world.

---

[1] A. Berkeley Mickelsen, *Interpreting the Bible* (Grand Rapids, MI: Eerdmans, 1977), 5.

[2] Thomas W. Africa, *The Ancient World* (New York: Houghton Mifflin, 1969), 2.

[3] G. J. Wenham, *Genesis 1–15*, vol. 1, *Word Biblical Commentary* (Waco, TX: Word Books, 1987), 37.

[4] Stanley N. Gundry and A. F. Johnson, *Tensions in Contemporary Theology* (Chicago: Moody Press, 1976), 353.

[5] Nancy Forbes and B. Mahon, *Faraday, Maxwell, and the Electromagnetic Field* (New York: Prometheus Books, 2014), 217–18.

[6] Walter C. Kaiser Jr. *Toward an Exegetical Theology* (Grand Rapids, MI: Baker Book House, 1981), 131.

[7] Michael. S. Heiser, *The Unseen Realm* (Bellingham, WA: Lexham Press, 2015), 16.

[8] Gordon D. Fee and D. Stuart, *How to Read the Bible for All It's Worth*, 4th ed. (Grand Rapids, MI: Zondervan, 2003).

[9] Walter Kaiser and Moisés Silva, *An Introduction to Biblical Hermeneutics: The Search for Meaning* (Grand Rapids, MI: Zondervan, 2007).

CHAPTER 5

Examples of Hermeneutical Problems

In a recent televised debate (2014) between Bill Nye (the Science Guy) and Ken Ham from the Answers in Genesis (AIG) ministry, Bill Nye was asked what would it take to convince him that the earth was young, that is, less than ten thousand years old. Mr. Nye responded that all he would need was "just one piece of evidence, just one." Here was a great opportunity for the YECs and Ken Ham to lay the whole matter to rest. So what did Ken Ham have to say in response to Bill Nye's comment? Mr. Ham did not supply any evidence of a young earth that would stand up to scientific scrutiny. Instead the only response Mr. Ham could make was to assert that he believes the literal interpretation of the English Bible, word for word. Did it ever occur to Ken Ham that perhaps his interpretations of the Bible may be wrong?

Let's spend a moment discussing the principal problem in biblical hermeneutics, that is, the principles of biblical interpretation. The underlying problem is that most church people will read the Bible as if it is a letter written to them personally, and they readily interpret it as such. Generally, most Bible readers find themselves reading the scriptures as they would most twenty-first-century literature. The failure in simply doing so is a lack of understanding the era in which the scripture was written. To properly understand the message of the Holy Word requires that the reader put on the character, nature, understanding, and life of the original intended reader. For example, the apostle Paul wrote the book of Romans to the young and struggling church in first-century Rome

(Romans 1:7,8). He did not write it to us in today's world. However, most of the message in Paul's letter to the Roman church still applies to us.

How would the Hebrew people, set free from Egypt in 1400 BC, react if Moses told them that the land (or earth) on which they stood was actually a giant ball eight thousand miles in diameter, turning on its axis with the velocity at the equator, spinning about one thousand miles per hour, and that it was whirling through an infinite universe at thirty-seven thousand miles per hour around the sun, which is ninety-three million miles away? I believe the Hebrew tribes, following Moses in the desert, would not have any idea what he was talking about. They may have decided that Moses was crazy. Perhaps they would have believed Moses if he had told them that the water for which they so desperately longed in their desert travels was nothing more than two parts hydrogen and one part oxygen.

Now let's get serious for a moment. Do you really believe that God would have spoken to the Hebrew refugees in a twenty-first-century AD language and cultural style? Absolutely not! God had to speak to these refugees in a language and cultural style that they would understand. That means God would have to *accommodate* their view of a stationary, flat earth, with a solid sky dome or vault above their heads, and also with the understanding that water is one of the four fundamental elements of the world, that is, water, air, earth, and fire. This idea of four elements was commonly understood by the ancients. Those wandering Hebrews knew nothing of the periodic table of elements. Theirs was the common understanding of the material world back in the days of the patriarchs.

So when we read the Bible and struggle to understand some of the more difficult passages, let us not forget this simple truth: God had to reveal Himself and His works in the language and cultural style of the people, in their time, if there was any chance of their understanding. This concept does not in any way violate the doctrine of biblical inerrancy. Inerrancy applies to the principles that the text affirms, such as the omnipresence of God, but it does not apply to the concepts of science, because the biblical text does not affirm the physics or science of the natural world. These things are just not applicable to the message of scripture. I want to be very clear on this point: I do not intend to question the concept of biblical inerrancy. Inerrancy does not apply to issues of scientific physical nature unknown to the ancient Near East. The Bible is *not* a physics or chemistry handbook. It was never intended to be that.

Figure 5.1 contains examples of problems with errant literal interpretations, along with my corresponding comments. I do not wish to impugn the authority of scripture; I only desire to illustrate the simple fact of accommodation when God led His disciples to write to His people thousands of years ago in a time and culture totally foreign to us as twenty-first-century readers.

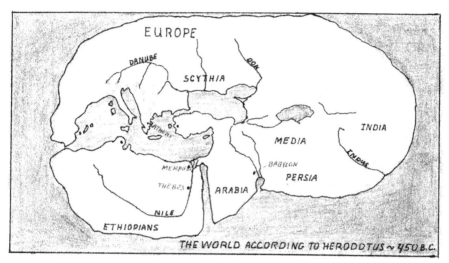

FIGURE 5.1 THE WORLD OF HERODOTUS

"All," "whole," or "entire" (as adjective or adverb). In scripture, when we read verses that seem to exaggerate the truth, must we ask the question, does *all* always mean *all?* How about Luke 2:1, where Caesar ordered that all the inhabited world should be registered for the purpose of taxation? Of course this order included the Incas, Aztecs, Cherokee, and Navajo Indians, and all the tribes in North and South America. Can you just imagine the Navajo Indians building boats so that they could sail to Rome in order to obey Caesar (pun intended)? There are dozens of biblical passages that use the word *all* or *whole* as a form of hyperbole. The reader needs to understand this concept. Is it simply a metaphor, or is it accommodation of the ancients' view concerning the size of the earth?

Did the apostle Paul really mean the *whole* world when he wrote to the Roman church in Romans 1:8 that their faith was being proclaimed throughout the whole world? Did the first-century Celts, Indians, Saxons, or Africans know about a church thousands of miles away in Rome? Or is this just another metaphor, an example of hyperbole? If Paul was correct, we do not need missionaries today, because the whole world has already been evangelized.

It would help the reader to see a map of the earth as understood by the ancient occupants in the centuries before Christ. Please refer to figure 5.1. In the days of Moses, the known world would have been smaller than shown on this map, because Moses wrote about 1000 years before Herodotus made his map of the world. Notice that the known world at that time was limited to the Mediterranean and the Mesopotamian basins. Also note that the map extends to the Indus River in India. This was about the limit of Alexandria's conquest (about 330 B.C.) in the fourth century BC. So when we read in scripture statements that imply the "whole earth" or "all the earth," this map illustrates the meaning as understood by the ancients.

Genesis 6–8 describes the flood that God sent to destroy the evil generation that sprang up after Adam. We read in Genesis 6:17, "Everything that is on the earth shall perish" (see also Genesis 7:23). Many Bible believers claim these verses as proof that God covered the whole earth with water, even up to the tops of the highest mountains. However, it is important to read Genesis 10, where we read the list of nations that Moses believed were on the earth (at least during the time of Moses). We clearly see that Moses did not believe that the universal flood covered the whole globe and killed everyone, first, because he didn't know about the other people around the globe, like the Chinese or the Eskimos; second, because the Nephilim were on the earth before and after the flood (Genesis 6:4 and Numbers 13:33); and third, because the Bible says that the waters covered all the mountains, yet Noah could see the mountaintops (cf. Genesis 8:5,9).

How about Genesis 41:56–57: "When the famine was spread over *all the face of the earth*, then Joseph opened all the storehouses, and sold to the Egyptians; and the famine was severe in the land of Egypt. The people of *all the earth* came to Egypt to buy grain from Joseph, because the famine was severe in *all the earth*" (emphasis added). Does this mean that the folks from Alaska or Argentina traveled to Egypt to buy food in 1800 BC?

Let's look at Acts 2:5: "Now there were Jews living in Jerusalem, devout men *from every nation* under heaven" (emphasis added). Was Luke (the author of the book of Acts) saying that Jews from North and South America, from China, and from Australia and India had traveled to Jerusalem for the Feast of Pentecost? I don't think so. Did people from all the earth flock to Jerusalem to seek the wisdom of Solomon? Turn to 1 Kings 10:24, where we read, *"All the earth* was seeking the presence of Solomon, to hear his wisdom which God had put in his heart" (emphasis added).

Now do you see the point that I am making? There are many other verses in scripture that use words of hyperbole, such as *all, whole,* and *entire,* to express a situation in the narratives. Check this out using your *Strong's Concordance* (preferably the one for the *NASB* version of the Bible). Does this make you wonder about the literal translation of the universal flood (Genesis 6–8), which some insist covered the *whole* earth (i.e., the entire planet)? Was it truly universal? Did it need to be universal to accomplish its purpose?

Flat earth. Does the Bible teach a flat earth, or does it teach that the earth is a sphere? An example of improper translation and interpretation is this verse in the paraphrase version of the Bible called *The Message,* where the translator took liberty to translate the word for "circle" as *ball:* "God sits high above the round ball of earth. The people look like mere ants" (Isaiah 40:22 MSG).

Compare this with the English Standard Version of the Bible, which reads: "It is He who sits above the circle of the earth" (Isaiah 40:22). The word *circle* is a translation of the Hebrew word *chug* (חוג), which should be translated as "circle" or "horizon" if in the noun form, or "to make a circle" or a "to draw a horizon circle" if in a verb form. In some places it is translated as "vault." The English word *vault,* which can mean "a dome or a covering" or "an arch," is not implied, and it most definitely does not mean "ball" or "sphere."

Let's look at a few other verses and decide what is meant by these words in scripture. In the book of Revelation we read, "After this I saw four angels standing at the *four corners of the earth"* (Revelation 7:1, emphasis added). And in Revelation 20:8 we read, "And will come out to deceive the nations which are in the *four corners of the earth*" (emphasis added). It is clear in these verses that the human author believed the earth was flat because he wrote that it had four corners. Another convincing verse from the Old Testament is Daniel 4:11, where we read, "The tree grew large and became strong and its height reached to the sky, and it was visible to the *end of the whole earth*" (emphasis added). It is clear that if a tree is visible to the ends of the earth, regardless of how tall it may be, this clearly implies that the earth had to be flat. And it is also clear that the writers of scripture believed in a flat earth as represented in the foregoing picture, Fig 5.1.

Now if you are thinking that I am criticizing the Bible, I want to make it perfectly clear that it was never God's intention to produce a holy book accurate in light of the known physical facts of the twenty-first century AD. In truth, for most of humankind's time on earth, excluding the last three or four hundred years, the belief in a flat earth was common. This may come as a surprise, but there are still residents of Earth who believe it is flat. Just check with Amazon.com for a list of currently available books explaining that the earth is actually flat. Ask some missionaries who have traveled to the far reaches of the planet in Africa, South America, New Guinea, and so forth. Would you like to be amused? There are still people in the civilized world who believe in a flat earth. Their numbers are dwindling, however. Even more amazing, there are people around the civilized world who believe in a "hollow" planet Earth because they believe that the hollow center is where the aliens keep all those flying saucers that some report seeing and that amuse others. It is hard to understand that there are intelligent people who still believe foolish things like this. Just visit an occult bookstore and check the literature on the shelves if you don't believe me.

Stationary earth. Does the literal interpretation of the Bible imply that the earth does not move? Well, Galileo believed that the earth circles the sun, and this is one of the reasons that the Catholic Church sought to kill him. You see, in those days the official church, as well as most Bible believers, held to the concept of a universe where the earth was in the center and everything else revolved around it, for example, the sun, moon, and stars. What does a literal interpretation of the Bible say? The Bible says that the earth does not move. Consider the following verses:

- "Tremble before Him, all the earth; Indeed, the world is firmly established, it will not be moved" (1 Chronicles 16:30).
- "Indeed, the world is firmly established, it will not be moved" (Psalm 93:1).
- "Indeed, the world is firmly established, it will not be moved" (Psalm 96:10).
- "He established the earth upon its foundations, So that it will not totter forever and ever" (Psalm 104:5).

So this leads us to our fourth point.

The sun stands still. In Joshua 10:12–13, we read that Joshua asked the Lord to stop the sun from going down because the warriors of Israel were in battle with the Amorites and more daylight time was needed for the army of Israel to be victorious. This verse relates to the concept of a stationary and flat world. It was believed in the days of the explorer Christopher Columbus that the world was flat and stationary and that the sun, moon, and stars revolved around the earth. Columbus had a difficult time convincing his sailors that if he sailed far enough to the west, they would not fall off the world, and that was in AD 1492. Because it was commonly believed years ago that the sun revolved around the earth, this verse posed no problem to the Bible readers of that day.

But let's examine this event with a more enlightened understanding of the actual mechanics of the solar system. First, we know that the sun doesn't move relative to planet Earth. It is the earth that travels around the sun in a circuit every 365 days (one year). Next, we know that it is the 24-hour daily rotations of the earth that give the appearance that the sun, moon, and stars are revolving around the earth. So it wasn't the sun that stood still when Joshua prayed to the Lord; it would have been the earth that came to a screeching halt. Since we know that the earth has a radius of about 4,000 miles, and that any point on the equator of the earth rotates one full rotation in 24 hours, we can calculate the tangential velocity of any point on the planet. The circumference of the earth at the equator has to be equal to two times the radius times Pi (that is 3.1415926 …). Let's plug that into our calculator and see what we come up with. The circumference at the equator is equal to $2\pi \times 4{,}000$ miles (the radius), or about 25,000 miles, so that is how far you would travel if you decided to fly around the earth at the equator. Knowing that one day is equal to 24 hours, the velocity of the earth at the equator must be 25,000 miles divided by 24 hours, or about *1,047 miles per hour*. I'll bet that most folks living in the tropics don't know that they are actually traveling that fast. But if you are flying in a fast military jet airplane, it would be possible to circle the earth, following the sun, and not see a sunrise or a sunset.

Now here is where it gets difficult. The land of Israel is not too far north of the equator, so we can approximate that Joshua and his army was standing on the surface of a planet that was spinning a little less than one thousand miles per hour. Now ask yourself, what would happen if the planet suddenly stopped spinning? Everything on its surface that wasn't tied down would go flying away, tangentially, at about one thousand miles per hour. That includes people, horses, chariots, trees, hills, temples, mountains, and of course, poor old Joshua. It the earth suddenly stopped rotating, the oceans would sweep across the continents at one thousand miles per hour, producing an unimaginable tsunami that would utterly destroy the whole planet and all life on it. Herein lies the next problem. The YECs would say that God momentarily changed the physical laws of momentum ($M_1 \times V_1 = M_2 \times V_2$, where M represents mass and V represents velocity). Why would God do something like that? And if He did, the side effects would alter the entire structure of the universe. Would it be more probable that God merely placed an angelic light in the sky that looked like the sun and brightened the battlefield for the army of Israel to be victorious? I believe this is what Joshua saw, and he reported it as being the sun because he didn't know any better. Nevertheless, it was a miracle of God. I hope the reader understands that all Bible students must interpret scripture using knowledge of ancient presuppositions and physical possibilities.

Ancient words for "earth," "ground," "planet," "universe," "mountain," and "hill." Do the ancient languages distinguish between *earth, ground, land, planet,* and *universe*? No, the only words used in the Old Testament for "land" are *eretz* and *adama*, and both of these words are used to refer to the land around the people, or the Promised Land by covenant, or the dirt under the people's feet. These words do not refer to a planet, just to the visible land upon which the people traveled. The ancients had no word for the planet on which we live. The ancient Hebrews had no concept or understanding of the world on which they lived as being a lonely planet suspended in empty space. Therefore, when the Bible refers to the universal flood (the flood of all the earth), there is no reason to understand that these verses apply to Asia, Africa, North and South America, the Antarctic and Europe.

The description of the flood says that the waters covered all the mountains (*har*) (Genesis 7:19). The word could also be used to mean a hill as well as a mountain. There is nothing in the text to suggest that the Himalayan Mountains were covered, including Mount Everest at twenty-nine thousand feet high. From the biblical perspective, Noah's flood accrued in the Mesopotamian plains between the Euphrates and the Tigris Rivers where there are no mountains, just hills, some a little bigger than others. When the text refers to all the earth being covered with water, there is no way one can understand the Bible as meaning the entire planet Earth. The word *eretz* (meaning earth, land, territory) was never used to refer to a planet, just the known flat land surrounding the people. Every time you read the word *earth* in Genesis, don't assume that the author is thinking of a huge spherical ball in space, our planet.

When the Old Testament writers talked about the "heavens and the earth," they were referring to the universe as they knew it—the sky above (including the abode of the gods in the third heaven) and the land beneath their feet. There is no word for "universe," as we understand it, in the ancient Hebrew language or in the Bible.

Universal death when Adam sinned. Paul wrote that *all* died in Adam. "Therefore, just as through one man sin entered into the world, and death through sin, and so death spread to all men, because all sinned" (Romans 5:12).

> "For since by a man came death, by a man also came the resurrection of the dead. For as in Adam all die, so also in Christ all will be made alive" (1 Corinthians 15:21–22).

Does this verse mean that following Adam's sin, every living thing on planet Earth came under the sentence of death, and that before Adam's sin there was no death? Did everything die when Adam sinned? The YECs claim that the result of Adam's sin was the sentence of death on all creatures of God, including the dinosaurs. (One YEC claimed on YouTube that the sentence of death following Adam's sin even included the foliage, that is, grass and trees.) Therefore, the YECs must believe that all creatures were created with "eternal life," since death was only the result of Adam's sin. Simply put, without sin entering into the world, all life would have been eternal.

If that is the case, then why did God plant the tree of life in the Garden of Eden? And why did He kick Adam and Eve out of the garden to prevent them from eating the fruit of the tree of life following their sin (Genesis 3:22–24)? The answer is that Adam and Eve and all other living things on the planet were not created with the purpose of physically living forever on earth. Only humankind had the provision to eat of the tree of life and live forever. Notice that we see the tree of life again in Revelation 22:2,14,19. The tree of life in the Garden of Eden was proof that humankind could not live forever, but needed the tree to maintain eternal life. Nothing is said about the animals needing to eat of the tree of life or having access to it.

Did dinosaurs eat grass and dwell with human beings before the Fall as claimed by Ken Ham and his creation museum (Answers in Genesis)? Then why do many dinosaur fossils contain teeth that are like sharks' teeth, used for tearing, ripping, shredding, and not for chewing or grinding as would be required for eating grass and leaves from trees? Look closely at figure 5.2, a picture of a dinosaur skeleton found in the museums.[1]

This is one of the strangest mistakes of the YECs when they are faced with the dinosaur problem. The fossil record clearly shows through thousands and thousands of samples that dinosaurs (giant lizards) actually lived on this planet, but since the YECs believe that our planet, Earth, is relatively young, they need to place the dinosaurs alongside early humankind, namely, Adam and Eve. So the Answers in Genesis (AIG) ministry tell us that Adam and Eve cohabitated with the dinosaurs safely because dinosaurs were herbivores and not carnivores (meat eaters). In fact the AIG shows this in their museum. So please explain to the world how dinosaurs could eat grass with those great big teeth that look to be designed to tear, rip, slice, and cut living flesh?

FIGURE 5.2 A DINOSAUR SKULL

AIG has a real problem explaining this. Furthermore, let me add that dinosaur bones are fossils made up mostly of silicon compounds and there is little to no calcium carbonates (bone material) left as found in normal bones. The reason is simple. The bones are very, very, very, very old (somewhere between 65 million and 250 million years old), and in the decomposition process, silicon compounds and other minerals replaced the calcium molecules in the structure of the bones so they are no longer real bones but principally stone.

Finally, I would like to mention a blessing left by the dinosaurs and other animal and plant life from millions of years ago: *oil, coal,* and *natural gas.* God gave us the energy that we need for our modern world when He created these giant lizards and other animals and plant life, because when they perished millions of years ago, they decomposed into petroleum (tar, pitch), coal, and types of methane gas, products which we use to power our modern world. Without such products we would still be living in a pre-civilized world, or as some would say, a stone age. This was all part of God's plan when He killed off the dinosaurs sixty-five million years ago. Another miracle!

Eating of flesh forbidden. In Genesis 4:4 we read that Abel offered an acceptable sacrifice of his flocks. The text says: "Abel, on his part also brought of the firstlings of his flock and of their fat portions. And the Lord had regard for Abel and for his offering."

So many have reported that the Bible teaches that humankind (including Adam and Eve) could only eat fruit and vegetables. This argument is based on Genesis 9:3, where we read: "Every moving thing that is alive shall be food for you; I give all to you, as I gave the green plant."

Now the question is: What did Abel do with the rest of the lamb that he slaughtered for the sacrifice? Did he eat it or burn it or throw it away? Anthropologists have for many years found animal bones in abandoned caves that were once used by early humankind as a principal dwelling place. They have also found charred remains of fire, which was used to prepare animal flesh for eating. And despite the false claims of the YECs, these cave dwellings have been dated as existing many thousands of years before the proposed dates of creation given by Bishop Ussher. For example, the city of Jericho has been dated as far back as 7000 BC.[2] In conclusion, I wish to add that radiometric dating (principally carbon-14) is and has been proven to be very accurate, despite what the YECs claim. Therefore the dates given for these archaeological finds can be accepted as the truth.

Gold as perishable. The Bible in 1 Peter 1:7,18 says that gold is perishable. Gold is a very stable element, a nonreactive metal. It is almost always found in its pure state. It doesn't change; therefore, it is not perishable. It's an almost inert element! Gold does not unite with any common elements such as oxygen to form a chemical compound, and therefore it cannot "rust" like iron or copper. Is this an example of "accommodation"? I believe so. However, jewelry that is made of gold can perish by continued usage, wear and tear, etc., so that it loses its luster, but the gold almost always remains inert, unchanged, and pure in chemical form. That is the principal reason it is so highly valued. Remember, Peter did not know about the chemical periodic table, so there was no way that he could have known about or understood atomic chemistry.

Biblical chronologies. The chronologies listed in the book of Genesis, chapters 5, 10, and 11, have been used by the YECs to prove that the universe and all that is in it was created approximately six thousand years ago. Despite the overwhelming evidence to the contrary, they remain dogmatically fixed in their interpretations. There have been volumes written by Old Testament scholars showing that the chronologies in the Bible were not written for the purpose of establishing age, but to show the legal lineage of the principal Old Testament characters, beginning with Adam and ending with Christ. It is obvious that I can't quote all of them here, as that would take hundreds of pages that many would not bother to read, so let me quote from a few of the most respected evangelical fundamentalist scholars. I believe their testimony should be sufficient.

One of the most prominent biblical scholars from the nineteenth century, Benjamin B. Warfield, wrote the following:

> The most influential of these chronological schemes is that which was worked out by Archbishop Ussher in his *Annales Veteri et Novi Testamenti* (1650–1654), and it is this scheme which has found a place in the margin of the Authorized English Version of the Bible since 1701. According to it, the creation of the world is assigned to the year 4004 B.C.[3]
>
> But for the whole space of time before Abraham, we are dependent entirely on inferences drawn from the genealogies recorded in the fifth and eleventh chapters of Genesis. And if the genealogies supply no solid basis for chronological inferences, it is clear that we are left without Scriptural data for forming an estimate of the duration of the ages. For aught we know they may have been of immense length. … The chronological suggestion is thus purely the effect of the arrangement of the names in immediate sequence; and is not intrinsically resident in the items of information themselves.[4]

Benjamin Breckinridge Warfield was professor of theology at Princeton Seminary from 1887 to 1921, and was considered by most to be a conservative theologian and the last of the great Princeton theologians before the liberal vs. fundamental split. Professor Warfield concluded in his writings that Bishop Ussher failed in his interpretation of the genealogies of Genesis and consequently failed to date the creation of the universe from them.

The well-known Bible scholar Gleason L. Archer stated in his survey of the Old Testament, "On the basis of internal evidence, it is the writer's conviction that 'yom' in Genesis One could not have been intended by the Hebrew author to mean a literal twenty-four hour day."[5] The conclusion of the majority of biblical scholars is that the genealogies of Genesis 5 and 11 were not meant to be used as date settings, but simply as a recording of the lives and names of the biblical patriarchs and the lineage to Christ.

Another suggestion for the list of names is that among the ancients was the popularity of the religious worship of one's ancestors. We see examples of this in 2 Kings 23:24: "Moreover, Josiah removed the mediums and the spiritists and the *teraphim* and the idols and all the abominations that were seen in the land of Judah and in Jerusalem, that he might confirm the words of the law which were written in the book that Hilkiah the priest found in the house of the Lord."

The "teraphim" were idols that represented one's ancestors. Refer to Genesis 31, where Rachel stole the family idols from her father, Laban, and caused a great rift in the family. This practice of having idols was forbidden by God, yet it flourished for centuries.

Falling stars. The Bible makes mention of falling stars in Daniel 8:10, Matthew 13:25, and Revelation 6:13 and 8:10. For thousands of years people assumed that the stars that they saw in the sky at night were pinpoints of light or angels. They did not know that the sun was a star, or that any of the stars that they saw in the sky were in fact millions of times bigger than the land on which they stood. Even the smallest star in the universe would obliterate our planet should it fall on us. It is obvious that the term "falling stars" was used by God to describe a great calamity that was coming someday to earth. This language is another example of God's accommodation of humankind's ignorance prevalent in those ancient days. Of course ancient human beings were familiar with "shooting stars," and on occasion they may have seen the damage caused by one of these meteors that hit the land beneath their feet, so the writer of the scriptures was correct in communicating the coming tragedies that awaited the lost world. But the expression "falling stars" is another example of the text that cannot be taken literally.

A matter of days: twelve hours, twenty-four hours, or an extended period of time. It is estimated that Moses wrote the Pentateuch during the forty years of wandering with the children of Israel after their release from captivity in Egypt. That would place the date of writing at about 1400 BC. If we properly understand the time sequence in the books of the Pentateuch, beginning with Genesis and ending with Deuteronomy, we must understand that the contents and characters of Genesis preceded the days of Moses. And therein lies our dilemma for the book of Genesis, because Moses was not a witness to the events of which he was writing.

Beginning with chapter 12, Genesis tells the story of Abraham and his descendants up to the time of their moving to Egypt. And there the story ends, until we read in Exodus of the events following the four hundred years' imprisonment of the Hebrew people in the land of Egypt. Beginning with Abraham, it is possible to roughly date the events in the Bible, but we are left with questions about dating the time before Abraham, that is, the first eleven chapters of Genesis. In Genesis chapters 5 and 10, we find lists of descendants going back to Adam, but there is no way to date these descendants without assuming that each one named followed the previous one sequentially with no lapsed time between any of them. The text of the scriptures does not give us any permission to establish dates by this method.

Many have tried to date the time of the beginning from these lists, but in doing so, they found that there are unexplained gaps in these genealogical lists that cannot be accounted for in reconstructing an ancient dating system. One must conclude that these genealogical lists were not intended to be used to calculate a date from the beginning. Nowhere in the Bible does one find attempts to determine dates based on the chronologies of Genesis. Based on the best scholarly estimates today, Abraham lived about 2000 BC (plus or minus one hundred years), and the Exodus from Egypt occurred about 1400 BC (some claim 1200 BC). Therefore, Moses was not alive during any of the episodes in Genesis, so he wrote the first book of the Bible based on common knowledge of his day, that is, Hebrew legends, folk tales, and perhaps some early historical writings. I'm not implying that these sources were incorrect or that Moses invented Hebrew history. We believe that God was also involved in directing Moses while writing the words of Sacred History. It is known that some of the episodes in the first part of Genesis are very similar to events recorded in other literature from ancient Near Eastern sources. A prime example is the common knowledge of the Great Flood.[6]

The scriptures teach us that God inspired the authors of scripture and that all that was written is without error (1 Timothy 3:16; 2 Peter 1:21). Now we need to look at the issue of time. How did the ancient people keep track of time prior to 2000 BC? Back then, the smallest unit of time was not the second, minute, or hour; it was the "day." The idea of a day could refer to the time of daylight or the time from sunrise to the next sunrise, or something in a similar order. Let me suggest that the idea of "day" in the ancient mind could also be used as a metaphor and refer to an unspecified unit of time. God may have used the word *day* to show that creation was a time-related process. Simply put, God was saying that creation happened over a period of time, sequentially, not instantaneously. Let's examine the following verse in reference to the matter of time:

The Lord God commanded the man, saying, "From any tree of the garden you may eat freely; but from the tree of the knowledge of good and evil you shall not eat, for in the *day* that you eat from it you will surely die." (Genesis 2:16–17)

But the man did not die! The man lived another nine hundred years according to the Hebrew text. Did God make a mistake? Did God lie? That is not possible. We read in scripture that God cannot lie, nor can He deceive (Numbers 23:19; 1 Samuel 15:29; Titus 1:2; Hebrews 6:18). Some will say that God was suggesting that Adam would die spiritually. Nowhere in scripture do we find a living person with a dead spirit. A person is a living soul made up of body and spirit. When the spirit leaves the body, the person is dead. Then what did God mean when He told Adam that he would die on the day he ate of the forbidden tree? Let us ask this question: when God used the word *day*, was He speaking in reference to humankind's domain (physical world, earth, universe), or was He using the word in reference to His heavenly realm? The question is, what is time in reference to God? The answer is provided in scripture, as follows:

- "For a thousand years in Your sight Are like yesterday when it passes by, Or as a watch in the night" (Psalm 90:4).
- "But do not let this one fact escape your notice, beloved, that with the Lord one day is like a thousand years, and a thousand years like one day" (2 Peter 3:8).

So these two verses imply that Adam did die on the day he sinned. It is just that the day was one thousand years long. Adam lived nine hundred and thirty years (the same day)—and then he died. Let's be sure to understand what these two verses say. Simply stated, these verses declare that God's time and timing is not the same as humankind's. Therefore we are faced with this fact concerning the use of the word *day* in the first chapter of Genesis. For some, the Bible seems to state that God made everything in six sequentially connected twenty-four-hour days, and then rested on the seventh day. In addition, many claim that the creation was completed just a little over six thousand years ago, based on the genealogical tables in the Bible, assuming for instance that there are no gaps in the genealogical lists. That is an improper assumption, because nowhere in scripture are we given permission to assume there are no gaps in these lists. The reader of scripture should not assume points of interpretation without first determining that such an assumption is permissible. James Oliver Buswell (1895-1977), a noted theologian and author, writes in his *Systematic Theology* the following: "As for the antiquity of man on the earth, we must bluntly say that the Bible gives us no data on which to base any conclusion or even any estimate."[7]

An important point to observe is that the definition of the length of a day is provided in Genesis 7:12, where it states that the rain fell for forty days and forty nights, implying that a day is only twelve hours. So which is it? Does the Bible define a day as twenty-four hours or as twelve hours, or as an extended period of time? I guess it would be correct to say, "Look at the context."

May I suggest that those adherents to the idea of a six-literal-day creation may not be aware of the Hebrew grammar in the first chapter of Genesis? An interesting fact arises when we read the Hebrew text of Genesis 1; the first five days in the text do not use a definite article, such as we would use, and translate with the word *the*, that is, "the first day," "the second day," "the third day," etc. Instead, each of the first five days are anarthrous, that is, with no definite article. Therefore the translation should be, "a first day," "a second day," "a third day," etc. Simply put, this form of grammar means that each of the first five days lacks *specificity*. I believe we can safely assume that this grammatical construction can only lead us to understand that these first five days are referring to an unspecified time period of an unspecified duration. However, days 6 and 7 have the definite article *the* included, and this changes the grammatical construction to imply something special. Humankind was created on day 6, and that begins history. It is also special in God's plan. Next, concerning day 7, according to Hebrews 4:4–6, this day still exists, and there is no mention of "evening and morning" as found relative to the other days. Simply put, day 7 is thousands of years long, and it is still ongoing.

Does the phrase "evening and morning" used for the first six days prove that these days must be only twenty-four hours long? Let us look at Psalm 90: "In the morning they are like grass which sprouts anew. In the morning it flourishes and sprouts anew; toward evening it fades and withers away" (Psalm 90:5–6).

This verse is using the idea of a day (twenty-four-hour period, evening and morning) to show how temporary life can be. This is an example of a figure of speech called a metaphor, because grass survives longer than twenty-four hours. Everyone needs to eat, don't they? If there is no grass, then there is no food for the animals.

Another example of the use of a metaphor with the word *day* is found in Genesis 31:23, where it states that Jacob fled from Laban, in the area of Haran, to the hills of Gilead, a distance of about three hundred miles, and that he took only seven days to complete the journey. Now, Jacob was traveling with a large herd of sheep, goats, camels, and donkeys, and with wives, servants, and children. If he only took seven days to cross three hundred miles of hill country that would mean that he traveled about forty-four miles per day. A modern army on foot with full field packs can only travel about twenty miles per day, so how did Jacob do it? The phrase "seven days" is an ancient metaphor for "a long time."

The prophet Hosea comforts Israel with this thought: "Come, let us return to the Lord. For He has torn us, but He will heal us; He has wounded us, but He will bandage us. He will revive us after two days;

He will raise us up on the third day, that we may live before Him" (Hosea 6:1–2).

The prophet is speaking of the restoration of the nation of Israel. That took a lot longer than three days, more like three thousand years, approximately. Then what is time for the LORD?

> "Remember His covenant forever, the word which He commanded to a thousand generations" (1 Chronicles 16:15).

If a generation is twenty years, then God is saying that He has kept His word a minimum of twenty thousand years. If a generation is forty years, then God has kept His word for forty thousand years. What happened to the six-day creation six thousand years ago? (Also see Deuteronomy 7:9 and Psalm 105:8.)

Looking at several different Bible translations, we see that the phrase "to a thousand" is also translated "for a thousand" depending on which version you are reading. But the key idea is the same, that is, God commanded His Word to/for a thousand generations of His people.

Another example of the Hebrew word for days *(yom)* being used for an extended period of time is found in Exodus 13:10; "Therefore, you shall keep this ordinance at its appointed time from year to year". Now this passage makes sense, because God is ordering Israel to observe the festival of Passover every year. However, in the Hebrew text on which this passage is translated we read; "you shall keep this law according to the times from days to days" [my translation]. In Young's Literal Translation of the Bible we read; "and thou hast kept this statute at its appointed season from days to days". Now what is it, years or days? The Hebrew word for "days" is יָמִימָה which is the plural form of *yom*יוֹם and is used twice in this verse referring to the regular observance of the feast of Passover that occurs once per year.

Moses, the author was using the word "days" to refer to an annual event that was an extended period of time of 360 days. This is additional proof that to a Hebrew the word "day" did not always mean a period of 12 hours or 24 hours, but instead a period of time determined by the context of the Scripture. In this case *yom* refers to a year of elapsed time. Now to affirm that this Hebrew text is not in error, let's check with the Greek Old Testament (Septuagint) where we find its translation reveals the same thing. The Greek text of Exodus 13:10 is; "καὶ φυλάξεσθε τὸν νόμον τοῦτον κατὰ καιροὺς ὡρῶν ἀφ᾽ ἡμερῶν εἰς ἡμέρας." My translation of this Greek text is; "and you shall keep this ordinance according to the times from days onto days". It seems that Young's translation is the only English translation that strove to translate accurately.

I Trust that this and the other examples in this chapter clearly show that to the ancient Hebrew, the word "day" did not always mean a time of 12 or 24 hours. Actually, the word "day" was often used to describe an unspecified period of time.

I hope the reader clearly sees that my purpose in this chapter is not to criticize the Bible but to explain that the words of the Bible were not written to us in the twenty-first century. These are things that God wrote to a very, very, very ancient people wandering in the desert. God's purpose was to tell these wanderers about their history and their God, the one and only true God. However, the message of this portion of the Bible is clearly meant to be a lesson and instruction to all believers for all eternity. In this the biblical message is for us today, clearly without error.

Next let us look at the overwhelming evidence that clearly show God's creation happened a long time ago.

---

[1] I have received permission from the Hot Springs County Pioneer Museum to add this picture to this book. I want to thank them for their kindness. I would encourage everyone going to Wyoming to stop by 700 Broadway St., Thermopolis, Wyoming, and visit their museum. I have been there twice and I would like to go again. They have a large display of dinosaur skeletons for public viewing and a large gift store and bookstore. Also, visit some of their restaurants and enjoy some genuine western country dining.

[2] Howard F. Vos, *Archaeology in Bible Lands* (Chicago: Moody Press, 1977), 180.

[3] B. B. Warfield, *Biblical and Theological Studies* (Philadelphia: Presbyterian and Reformed Publishing Co., 1968 [reprint]), 239.

[4] Warfield, 240, 244.

[5] Gleason L. Archer, *A Survey of Old Testament Introduction* (Chicago: Moody Press, 1977), 186.

[6] G. Herbert Livingston, *The Pentateuch in Its Cultural Environment* (Grand Rapids, MI: Baker Book House, 1974), 89.

[7] James O. Buswell, *A Systematic Theology of the Christian Religion*, vol. 1 (Grand Rapids, MI: Zondervan, 1977), 325. Dr. Buswell was well-known among conservative theologians as the dean of Covenant College and Seminary, Saint Louis, Missouri. He was the author of many theological books, earned many degrees in biblical theology, and served in numerous academic positions during his lifetime.

CHAPTER 6

Evidence That Demonstrates Universal "Old Age"

When Albert Einstein discovered the physical law related to the equivalence of matter and energy, he did not discover something new, but only a truth created by the God of our universe, because *all truth is God's truth*. Keep this in mind as we examine how we can know for certain the relative age of God's creation, that is, the age as we are able to perceive it. In this chapter, my primary purpose is to explain why much of the modern world accepts or understands that the universe is very old while there is still a large minority of people in the United States who will not accept the findings of modern scientific research, but instead insist on the old ideas that the universe and all that is in it was created on a special day about six thousand years ago.

The young earth creationists (YECs) tend to seek any way possible to fit applicable scientific facts into a young earth scenario. In some situations, I have discovered that they have even gone so far as to distort actual proven scientific data to prove their point. Why is this so? I think it stems from the idea that many people find science to be a very boring subject of study and have avoided it in school and life. When some of our citizens find an article explaining how scientists have discovered data that demonstrates the true age of our world, they pass over it because they lack scientific understanding and interest in a subject that requires deep thought. Perhaps the problem lies with our educational system. As currently reported in many venues, American youth today continue to fall behind the rest of the world in science and math knowledge, as seen in the following article from *USA Today*.

The Associated Press, New York, December 10, 2010, 2:55 p.m.

> United States students are continuing to trail behind their
> peers in a pack of higher performing nations, according to
> results from a key international assessment. Scores from
> the 2009 Program for International Student Assessment
> to be released Tuesday show 15-year-old students in the
> U.S. performing about average in reading and science,
> and below average in math. Out of 34 countries, the U.S.
> ranked 14th in reading, 17th in science and 25th in math.
> Those scores are all higher than those from 2003 and
> 2006, *but far behind the highest scoring countries*, including
> South Korea, Finland and Singapore, Hong Kong and
> Shanghai in China and Canada.

In light of this situation, I will strive in this chapter to point to specific
well-known data showing the true age of God's creation, and at the same
time I will try to explain the data sufficiently so that, without a scientific
background, most will be able to understand. It is not necessary for me
to produce one thousand items of evidence for an old universe (even
though enough evidence does exist), but I am only required to produce
one irrefutable piece of evidence that God created everything long before
Bishop James Ussher (1581–1656) calculated the date of creation from
the chronologies in the English Bible. In the rest of this chapter I plan
to describe a reasonable number of irrefutable items that clearly show
Bishop Ussher was wrong. The earth and the universe were not created
on October 23, 4004 BC.

At this point I want to add a comment from a well-known scientist,
David Montgomery (PhD in geology): "If we embrace the claim that
earth is a few thousand years old, we must also throw out the most basic
findings of Geology, Physics, Chemistry, and Biology."[1]

Dr. Montgomery is exactly correct. One cannot arbitrarily pick and
choose which scientific methods and data to use in determining reality. Let
me begin with an important concept that upset the scientific community
to the core. Up to the middle of the twentieth century, scientists generally
believed that the universe was eternal, with no beginning and no end.

However, with the revelation or, should I say, the discovery by astronomer Erwin Hubble in 1929 that the visible universe was expanding at an ever-increasing rate, a shock wave overtook the scientific community, because they had previously believed mostly in a static universe, that is, a universe eternal and fixed in size. Therefore, there was no need for a creator, in their opinion. Too many of the "intellectual thinkers" were upset that they may have to change their opinions about the universe, accept the idea of a creation, and admit to themselves and others that since the universe had a beginning; it must also have had a creator.

Originally Einstein was convinced of an eternal static universe, and he modified his equations of gravity from his General Theory of Relativity to fit this preconceived notion. Einstein and most other scientists agreed that the laws of gravity would require the universe to collapse in on itself in time. Therefore Einstein added a factor to his equation called the "gravitational constant" that was able to change the formula to agree with his opinion that gravity would not force the universe to collapse into itself at any time. Later, when provided with the proof of a "creation" instance and an expanding universe, Einstein corrected his equation and admitted that his modification was the worst mistake of his career. The universe really did have a beginning! As a result of Hubble's discovery, and Einstein's new equation of gravity, scientists were forced to accept that the universe had a beginning, and many of them were forced to accept the idea of a creator, some against their desired opinion. The evidence has shown conclusively that not only did the universe have a beginning, but also that it began as nothing but an infinitely small point, and from that dimensionless point all matter, energy, time, and space were created. The result was an ever-expanding universe. In other words, everything that now exists came from nothing, except from the mind of God. And this is exactly what the Bible proclaims!

Just look at these following verses where the Bible clearly teaches that everything that now exists came from nothing: John 1:3, Romans 4:17, Colossians 1:16, Hebrews 11:3, and Revelation 4:11. The singular difference, however, is that the Bible does not date the beginning. So the question lingers: why do the YECs make such a big deal out of a presupposed date of creation? Do they suppose that the authenticity of the Bible depends on their success in proving that the universe is just six thousand to ten thousand years old? Do they believe that this goal justifies their lack of proof when they critique proven physical facts of the universe? Do they believe that somehow their disparagement of proven physical facts showing the actual age of the universe will somehow win their acceptance from our Lord? Their insistence on "made-up" science and physics is very sad, at the least, and does not further the cause of the gospel.

Obviously, the Hubble discovery led to a dilemma concerning a creation from nothing among the scientific community, which had previously held that there was no creation, and therefore any discussion concerning a creator god was irrelevant. Please understand that the evidence that currently exists proving our created universe is very, very, very old makes up an extremely long list, containing perhaps thousands of items. However, I plan to share with the reader a number of irrefutable facts and list some of the most prevalent proofs of old age. I might warn the reader that the YECs spend a lot of their time dreaming up answers to explain away the evidence that I am about to list. The YECs have even gone so far as to invent new science as a way of explaining and dismissing the evidence of an old universe. They offer no proof except the argument that it had to be that way because the English Bible teaches that the universe was created in just a couple of days (no, actually, the Bible does not teach any such thing).

The rest of this chapter will be filled with a few of the many proofs for an old age of the earth and the universe. The point that I would like readers to keep in mind as they read from the following list is that there only needs to be one piece of irrefutable evidence to prove that the earth and the universe are very old.

Explaining a Nova Explosion and the Speed of Light

It may be of interest to some that light is actually a form of electromagnetic radiation (EMR). The only difference between light waves, radio waves, microwaves, x-rays, and gamma waves is just the frequency of the waves (we can use the word *rays* in place of *waves*). It should also be of interest to the reader that EMR is just pure energy. No one truly knows what it is or from what it is made. However, thanks to Albert Einstein (and much verified empirical data since), we now know that matter and energy are related to each other by the fixed constant, *c*, which represents the velocity of EMR (in this case, light) in free space, or about 300,000,000 meters per second, or 186,000 miles per second. This constant is the relation of matter to energy throughout all of God's creation and is described by the simple formula $E = mc^2$ or $c = \sqrt{E/m}$. This formula has been proven many times in laboratories and universities across the world in this last century; therefore, it would be ridiculous for me to add any proof in *And There Was Light*. I also proved this equation in my lab class called Engineering Physics while at the university from which I eventually graduated. So when God created light, He created all that was required to manufacture our universe and all that is in it. Light is energy, and remember, Einstein proved that energy can be converted to matter and vice versa.

So when God created light, He actually created everything that now exists in the universe. Scientists don't have all the answers, but it is accepted that matter and energy are interchangeable by known processes. As our nuclear bombs have proved, energy can be converted to matter and matter can be converted to energy. Perhaps the greatest discovery in this last century was that the universe had a beginning. This known beginning is often referred to as the "big bang." This term was originally created as a pejorative term to humiliate the finding that proved to the skeptical that the universe actually sprang into existence in an instant many billions of years ago. When God created light, He created what some refer to as the "big bang," that is, an instant explosion of light and matter that was created from nothing, from which all things now existing were formed. God spoke the words "let there be light" <u>and there was light</u>!

Now to address an important fact about this thing called *c*, or the velocity of light (a form of electromagnetic radiation or EMR). In free space, it is a universal *constant*. It can't be changed. The very structure of our universe would change if *c* could be changed. Let me show how this applies. The final term in Einstein's gravitational equation is $(8\pi G)/c^4$. Einstein did not invent this term; he discovered it as it is in God's creation. What this term says is that if the YECs are correct, in order for God to have created everything in just a few days, the velocity of light in the beginning would have to be infinite. This is what some YECs argue to support their claim that it didn't take 2.5 million years for light from the Andromeda galaxy to reach earth because God speeded it up to an infinite velocity during the creation week and light reached all points in the universe instantly during creation. However, according to this gravity equation, there was no gravity in the universe, because the above term goes to zero (0) if c goes to infinity (∞). The universe could not exist. I can't explain it any further than to say that the velocity of EMR (light, radio waves, cosmic rays, etc.) is constant for every observer, regardless of relative velocities. This was a fact proven by the Michelson and Morley experiments in 1881.[2] So the YECs have to guess again and hope they can fit their preconceived notions of creation into their misunderstanding of the text of the English Bible.

On August 8, 2007, astronomers discovered in the Vega constellation a new supernova, V458.[3] The distance of the supernova was calculated by a "constant, standard candle" principle of illumination at a distance. Based on the knowledge that V458 was a type 1a supernova that had a known light output, astronomers calculated that the supernova was 13 kiloparsecs away, or about 42,380 light years away from Earth. One light year is the distance that light can travel in one year, knowing that light still travels at 186,000 miles per second. Therefore, when the supernova exploded, we were still in one of the ancient ice ages, about 42,000 years ago. But according to the YECs, the earth and the universe didn't exist at that time.

On February 23, 1987, a new supernova (SN1987a) was discovered near the outskirts of the Tarantula Nebula in the Large Magellanic Cloud. The Large Magellanic Cloud can be seen in the Southern Hemisphere with the naked eye and is considered a mini galaxy outside our Milky Way galaxy. The distance from Earth was calculated by the standard candle method to be approximately 167,000 light years from Earth. In other words, the light from this very bright supernova (which could be seen by the naked eye on Earth) took 167,000 years to reach us. But according to the YECs, the earth and the universe didn't exist at that time.

One of my hobbies is amateur astronomy. I have a large "backyard" telescope that I use on occasion to view the evening skies. Years ago, in the middle of an autumn evening, I discovered the galaxy called Andromeda with my scope. That was a special moment for me to see that distant galaxy with my own eyes. As I pondered the view, I could not help but think that I was looking at some of God's creation 2,500,000 light years away. It takes 2.5 million years for the light from Andromeda to reach us here on Earth. Totally mind-boggling! But according to the YECs, Earth and the universe didn't exist at that time. So what was I looking at? Now the YECs claim that God created light in motion; that is, light would have been created already in motion, most of the way to planet Earth, so that it would appear to us as a long time in transit, but actually a short time according to the YECs. That claim would make God to be a deceiver, whose only purpose was to prove that the YECs' interpretation of the English Bible was correct all along. I can't accept that conclusion.

The value of c in free space is a constant. The actual value of c (as mentioned above) has been discovered in the exploration of our natural world. Another example where c shows up is in the physical strength of the interaction between a charged particle and a photon. This value is called the "fine structure constant"[4] and is equal to $2\pi e^2/hc$. Notice that our universal constant, c, is included in this mathematical relationship. This was not designed by humankind; it was discovered by humankind. It was created by God that way. Now if the value of c has changed as the YECs attest, just so that they could make an excuse that the earth is only six thousand years old, then c would have to be almost infinite, the "fine structure constant" term would approach zero, and there would be no strength to hold the subatomic particles together. Therefore, all atoms would collapse and disappear. There would be no earth, no universe.

The value c appears in many other equations dealing with atomic particles and radiation or wave field theory. This is where it gets interesting. What I am about to write is taken from a typical college textbook on engineering physics.[5] Michael Faraday, a British scientist who lived in the nineteenth century, performed many tests and experiments over his lifetime. His work was principally concerned with the mysteries of electricity, a yet unknown phenomenon. By the mid-nineteenth century, a young mathematician, James Clerk Maxwell, worked on all the experimental data that Faraday had collected and started a serious study of electrical and magnetic fields—a new and mysterious subject in his day.

About the same time, other scientists had developed standard values for some mathematical constants that that had been discovered. It was necessary to unify the physical findings into a scientific metric system, as we now use today. The system is known as the MKS system of units, or in simple words, the meter, kilogram, and second system of units. In time, experimenters discovered that there was a constant magnetic permeability in all their experiments, and they wrote it as μ. Its measured value was 8.854×10^{-12} in free space. The experimenters discovered that there was an electric field associated with the magnetic field, and there was measured another value, this time the permittivity constant of free space, which they wrote as ε. Its measured value is 1.256×10^{-6}. You can verify these values in most college textbooks on Physics.

Now the facts get exciting. James Maxwell continually ran into a problem while working with Faraday's data. As Maxwell continuously worked by configuring equations to explain Faraday's lab work, he discovered a relationship that appeared repeatedly in his formulations. To keep this explanation short, I'll say it this way: Maxwell discovered that for some of his equations that he developed to describe the electrical–magnetic phenomena, he often found that the product of the permittivity constant and the permeability constant appeared under the square root radical, which was also inverted in a reciprocal term. Maxwell finally discovered that the mathematics was teaching him something. When he solved the radical term, he discovered c!

Maxwell discovered that these physical constants actually reveal the velocity of light or what is better known as *electromagnetic radiation*, EMR. This is the formula, $c = 1/\sqrt{\mu\varepsilon}$, and the resulting value, if one choses to work it out, is 299,792,458 meters per second, or about 300,000,000 meters per second, or in scientific shorthand, 3×10^8 meters per second— the velocity of light (or 186,000 miles per second), an electromagnetic radiation (EMR, light rays, radio waves, gamma rays, x-rays, microwaves, ultraviolet rays, etc.). It is a fixed constant and cannot be changed in free space.

So the YECs are still busy trying to compose another excuse to explain why c is always true and yet the universe is still only six thousand years old. One prominent young earth advocate (who holds a degree in astronomy from the University of Colorado) claims that when God created the universe, the velocity of EMR (light waves, radio waves, cosmic rays, etc.) was infinite in the direction toward the earth but half the value of *c* when going away from the earth. This special exception he referred to as the anisotropic synchrony convention. He is basically making the claim that we change the convention by which we measure the velocity of light. This idea is essentially the same as stating you will measure the area of your house using meters instead of yards. The answer will still be the same because the size of the house doesn't change. By making this "untested" claim, he assumes that he has answered the problem and has accounted for the literal creation of the entire universe a mere six thousand years ago. A further point he has ignored is the proven fact that the velocity of EMR to each observer in free space is exactly the same no matter how fast the observer is traveling, or in which direction any observer may be traveling. This proven fact is one of the great mysteries of creation, known by all who study the physics of the universe, but only understood by God.

It might interest the reader to know that both Faraday and Maxwell were devoted Christians who knew their Bible. "Like Faraday and like Newton, Maxwell believed that God made the universe, that the laws of physics were God's laws, and that every discovery was a further revelation of God's great design. At the same time, as a devout Christian, he believed that the true nature of God was to be found in the Holy Bible, which he knew as well as any scholar of divinity."[6]

One last detail to be remembered: humankind did not invent these formulas and relationships; humankind discovered them! God made the universe that way, and He created the formulas that we use. When we study our universe, we discover the formulas that God created. Let me add a word from the scriptures: the speed of EMR does not change, because "God's laws do not change" (Jeremiah 33:25)! The value of the speed of light (including all EMRs) is a root value throughout much of modern physics and cannot be changed without disrupting God's providential care of the universe and of humankind.

Expanding Universe and Hubble's Constant

For centuries, our Milky Way was considered the total universe. One simple reason was that the Milky Way was all that humankind could see with the naked eye. Then with the invention of the telescope, people were able to see more of the Milky Way, but they had no way of knowing that there was more out there. It wasn't until the turn of the twentieth century that larger telescopes allowed astronomers to see things that were not previously visible. Perhaps the biggest boom for astronomy was the building and installation of the giant hundred-inch telescope on Mount Wilson in Southern California in 1917. The second biggest boom was the employment of Edwin Hubble as the lead astronomer.

Hubble was a very diligent worker who dedicated himself to the task of defining the yet unknown fuzzy smears or clouds (called nebulae, meaning "cloud" in Latin) often seen in space through this new large telescope. In his many hours staring through the mighty hundred-inch telescope (the largest in the world at that time), Hubble was intrigued by the appearance of these fuzzy patches or clouds in space, one of which we now know as Andromeda. In his hours of viewing, Hubble discovered that one of the stars in the fuzzy cloud called Andromeda was changing in brilliance. He had found what is known as a Cepheid variable star. A Cepheid variable star has a unique feature that makes it valuable for determining distance. A Cepheid star varies in intensity at a frequency determined by its absolute illumination or light output. Therefore, a very bright Cepheid will vary its light output at a constant rate proportional to its absolute brightness, and a dim Cepheid star will vary its intensity at a different rate or frequency proportional to its absolute illumination. By measuring the frequency of the illumination of a Cepheid star, one is able to determine its absolute brightness. Astronomers can then determine the distance to the star using the inverse square law as a measure of distance. This is called a "standard candle" measurement.

After a long time period of months and years viewing and recording the brightness of some of the variable stars in Andromeda, Dr. Hubble was able to calculate the distance to Andromeda as approximately 2.5 million light years (a light year is the distance that light travels in one year—about 5.9 trillion miles) from our planet, Earth. By May 1935, Hubble published his results in the *Astrophysical Journal*, where he presented proof of his findings that showed that Andromeda was a separate galaxy from the Milky Way. Using the same procedures, Hubble also provided data for more of these nebulae showing many of them were other galaxies.

Now one of the tools that astronomers use in analyzing distant stars and other heavenly bodies is the technique known as spectrographic analysis. This is the process where an astronomer will examine the light from a distant body by taking a spectrograph of its light. The results tell the scientist the chemical composition of the distant body. Astronomers can use this information to predict the age of some of the stars. However, when Hubble used this technique, he discovered something quite unusual. For most of the galaxies that he viewed, the spectrograph showed a distinct shift of the received light to the red side of the light spectrum. This meant that the body under observation was moving away from us. This frequency shift is similar to what we call the "Doppler Shift" when we hear a train whistle change in sound or pitch as the train passes by us. The amount of "red shift" indicated the speed at which the body was moving. What Hubble concluded was that all visible galaxies (except the ones closest to us, called the "local group") were moving away from our Milky Way, and the farthest from us were moving the fastest. Hubble's data has been confirmed many, many times by astronomers over the last century. This discovery means that the universe is expanding at an ever-increasing rate. The farthest galaxies are moving away faster than the nearest galaxies. No one knows why; it is only that God created it that way.

Hubble's discovery led him to plot his data, where each data point on the graph represents a galaxy's distance from earth based on the amount of detected "red shift." An example of Hubble's chart or graph is seen in Figure 6.1. Please note that the vertical axis of the graph in figure 6.1 represents the velocity of the observed galaxy as it moves away from us, and the horizontal axis represents the distance of the same observed galaxy. Hubble discovered that the data actually gave an accurate indication of the age of the universe. Let me show the reader how this was done by using the figure 6.1 as an illustration. The data plotted in this graph was determined by measuring the red shift of many different galaxies, and it was found to closely fit a straight line by using the "least mean square" method of plotting experimental data. (The "least mean square" method of plotting data can be explained in most college math textbooks and is a procedure to determine the best fit of a line or a curve to experimental data.)

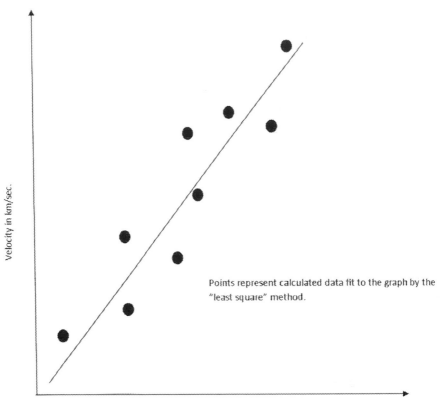

Points represent calculated data fit to the graph by the "least square" method.

Velocity in km/sec.

Distance in millions of light years

FIGURE 6.1 HUBBLE'S PLOT

Now the origin of this chart (the lower left-hand corner of figure 6.1) represents the beginning, year zero and distance zero. This chart is also represented by the formula H = V/D. The letter *H* is used to represent the slope of the best fit line as shown in the formula; it is also referred to as the Hubble constant. The letter *V* is the recessional velocity of the galaxy object in space, and the letter *D* represents the distance of the same galaxy object in light-years. Note that this graph is my own creation for the purpose of an illustration. However, Hubble's graph has been updated with many more galaxies many times since Hubble first calculated it, and much more recent data has been added. Now an interesting thing happens when we take the reciprocal of the Hubble equation. The graphed line represents velocity per years, but the reciprocal of the equation represents years per velocity. If we calculate from the beginning of the graphed line, we end up with a figure for the age of the universe, and that comes out to be about 14,000,000,000 years. This Hubble chart (or constant) is now used to determine the distance of all new galaxies that have been found, based on their observed red shift. The latest calculations on the age of the universe have been refined to about 13.76 billion years. Since we have determined that the universe had a beginning, we also must conclude, based on the above illustrations, that everything began in an instant from an infinitely small point or as it often referred to a "singularity" (i.e., zero mass and zero energy, or more exactly, the universe was created from nothing). Since this is true, the beginning of the universe must have left some evidence or some kind of electromagnetic noise that now still echoes throughout space. And this leads us into our next subject.

The Cosmic Background Microwave Radiation

Cosmologists (physicists who study the universe) have accepted Hubble's findings, but they came to the conclusion that if the universe was created in an instant as predicted, then there has to be some evidence of this event. The evidence could not have been a big bang because there is no sound in space. However, the instant of creation must have been a very noisy event—that is, noise that can be measured as an electromagnetic wave or emission. This idea was accepted for many years, but no one knew how to measure this noise. As it happened one day in 1965, two scientists for Bell Labs were conducting experiments on telephone satellite communications in an open field near Princeton University in New Jersey. They were irritated by the fact that all satellite communications were disturbed by an electrical background noise that interfered with normal communication attempts. As we all now know, long-distance phone conversations are made possible by our satellites that we use to carry our messages around the world.

The two Bell Lab scientists, struggling to find the source of their problem, tried every engineering trick they could think of to discover the problem. They were mainly confused about the source of the electrical noise, because no matter where they pointed their antenna, the noise persisted and was just as strong in all directions, up, down, left, and right. It just did not make sense to them. After several years searching for an answer, they came upon the solution that the electrical noise originated from everywhere—from space, and not from the earth, but from the space on the other side and beyond the earth. Later, measurements were made of this mysterious electrical noise, and it was found to be in the range of very high frequencies (VHF) to the microwave frequencies. Calculating the energy of these unknown radio frequency waves led them to a value of about 2.7° Kelvin. I want to keep this section short, so I won't go into great detail of the physics and mathematics, but I must conclude with this fact, that the radiation they discovered was exactly what was predicted earlier by those who had understood the initial creation event, also referred to as "the big bang".

If you own an old black-and-white TV with rabbit ears, you can see this noise for yourself. Just tune your TV to an empty channel, either channel 2 or 3, and you will see on the screen what we call "snow". About 10 percent of that snow on your TV is actually the radiation from the creation event 14 billion years ago. This creation event actually happened; the proof is there for all to see. We are surrounded by a cosmic background radiation field that is the result of God's initial creation. Since this discovery by the scientists Arno Penzias and Robert Wilson, several major satellites have been launched over the last fifty years for the purpose of measuring the level and distribution of this background radiation, and the results have continued to prove that this cosmic background radiation is truly that noise left over from creation. By the way, Penzias and Wilson won the Nobel Prize for their discovery. The whole scientific community now accepts this creation event as fact. Now the atheists and the YECs have a problem.

Explaining Radiometric Dating Methods

Every time I listen to a young earth creationist (YEC), I hear the same argument: "You can't trust carbon-14 dating results." Well, they are correct if they are referring to radiometric dating from many years ago when the science was still new. No doubt mistakes were made, but times and knowledge have changed things. As an example, many YECs like to point out the errors made in the early days of radiometric dating when scientists produced errors in dating sea creatures via C-14 means. Well, the error was quickly found when the scientists realized that sea creatures were not subjected to the same C-14 radiation as land-dwelling creatures. So for years, YECs loved to get a crowd of young Christians laughing during their lectures when they talked about some of the glaring errors made by scientists doing radiometric measurements. What the YECs fail to mention is that the results are now much more accurate because of many years of research and better testing equipment. In today's laboratories, testing for carbon-14 is much more involved for the purpose of reducing errors. Today's procedure requires more than one sample; usually many samples will be used to verify the approximate date of the material under examination. Then it must also be understood that carbon-14 tests are only applicable to matter that was once living and inhaling carbon from the atmosphere. That includes a list of organic material such as plants and foliage that lived above water, and living, breathing land-roaming creatures. You can't test rocks for age using the carbon-14 techniques.

Once I attended a lecture by a member of the Answers in Genesis ministry where the gentleman mentioned that you can't test rocks for age via the carbon-14 method. The audience responded with an "Ooh!" The fellow from AIG said, "See?!" He purposely left the audience believing that it was not possible to date rocks by any radiometric means. YECs seem to imply that if they discredit C-14 dating, then all radiometric dating is suspect. Wrong conclusion!

Not long ago I had the opportunity to listen to a lecture by a YEC. He made the claim that since the half-life of carbon-14 is only fifty-seven hundred years, there should not be any C-14 left on earth if the earth is billions of years old. His suggestion was simply that all C-14 should have disappeared by now. At first his question puzzled me, since this YEC had an advanced degree in astronomy, so he should have known the solution to the puzzle. Obviously there were people in his audience who didn't know the solution, so this suggestion brought a round of approval from the crowd, who, while laughing and cheering, obviously thought the speaker had scored a point in a serious debate. I was dumbfounded. The solution is simple: there are carbon atoms in the earth's upper atmosphere in the form of carbon dioxide and carbon monoxide, plus a few other compounds. The earth and its upper atmosphere are constantly being bombarded by cosmic rays from the sun and other sources from outer space. It is these cosmic rays that create the ions and isotopes in our upper atmosphere, and they also create C-14 that combines with other elements, forming compounds that are consumed by plants and animals living on the earth's surface. That is how the earth achieves a constant supply of C-14. That YEC knows this to be true, so why didn't he tell the public audience? Was he trying to hide something? Was he being deceitful?

The truth is simply that there are at present about forty different radiometric means of dating ancient material, including rocks. The YECs do not want this truth to get around. Let me list a few of the common isotopes used for radiometric dating of rocks and fossils.[7]

	Radioactive Isotopes	Half Life
1.	Uranium 238 – Lead 206	4.5 billion years
2.	Potassium 40 – Argon 40	1.26 billion years
3.	Uranium 235 – Lead 207	700 million years
4.	Uranium 234 – Thorium 230	248 thousand years
5.	Rubidium 87 - Strontium 87	48.8 billion years
6.	Carbon 14 – Nitrogen 14	5715 years
7.	Thorium 230 – Radium 226	75,400 years
8.	Beryllium 10 – Boron 10	1.52 million years

FIGURE 6.2 CHART OF RADIOACTIVE ISOTOPES

An explanation is needed at this point. All radionuclide isotopes, known to be unstable elements, will decay. The decay rate is constant. It cannot be changed, either by temperature, pressure, or any physical or chemical means. The decay rate is based on the nuclear binding strength of neutrons to the nucleus of the atom. This binding strength cannot change. It was fixed from creation. The YECs claim that the isotope rate of decay changed when Adam sinned. I have no idea where they came up with that idea. I believe they just made it up so they could provide an answer that would support their claim of a six-thousand-year-old universe.

So for any isotope, the radioactivity is the result of the nucleus losing neutrons at a fixed (constant) rate (in the decay process, the atom also emits some electrons, x-rays, and gamma rays). For many elements, this rate has been measured, and since this rate is an exponential rate (not a linear one), it is easier to use an exponential expression to indicate the rate of decay. Therefore, scientists have adopted the concept of what they call "half-life." One half-life is the time it takes for half the isotope to decay to the daughter material. Two half-lives is the time it takes for three-quarters of the material to decay to the daughter material, and so on, following the exponential rate of always half the remaining material. This means that there will always be a portion of the original material present, however small. However, it is accepted practice not to record dating that exceeds ten half-lives. So for carbon-14, this means that it is possible to collect good age data up to about fifty thousand years ago. I need to add another point: when scientists work on dating a sample of ancient material, they never use just one method. It is common practice to employ several dating methods, and if all the methods that were tried confirm a result by returning approximately the same date, then scientists can assume, rightly so, that they have a good answer.

The next wrinkle that YECs throw into their argument is that the decay process of radioisotopes produces what is normally called a "daughter" product. The percent of the original isotopes is called the "parent" material, since it is the "parent" that produces the "daughter" product through radioisotope decay. The question then becomes, how can a scientist know for sure that the original created material had no "daughter" product? Or let's state the problem differently: Can a scientist know for certain that the original material contained 100 percent parent material? The answer to these questions is a positive. Yes, trained lab technicians can and do successfully separate the percentages of "parent" and "daughter" products. However, I suppose that the YECs don't mention the methods that are used for fear that their failed logic will be suspect.

Fearing that the reader will accuse me of getting too technical, I believe it is necessary for me to divert for a moment to demonstrate the mathematics used to calculate the relationships between the decay process and the results of radiometric dating. The following logarithmic formula is well-known among those schooled in college physics. I taught a physics class many years ago, and I still remember the formula as $A = A_0 e^{kt}$, where A is the original abundance of the parent material, A_0 is the present abundance of the parent material, e is the base of the natural logarithm, k is the known half-life, and t is the elapsed time. Using this equation, it is possible to calculate the original amount of material. Now let me add, the task is not yet complete in that it will be necessary to repeat the test on more than one sample of the material in question. The test may need to be repeated three, four, five, or more times on the same sample, then the results, which are the ratio of daughter to parent material for each test, will need to be plotted on graph paper or on a computer. The calculated ratios should line up as a straight line (approximately). This line is called an isochron line, and the slope of this line gives the best value for the ratio of daughter to parent material, thereby resulting in a good approximation of the age of the sample in question. (If the reader has a difficult time digesting this explanation, please accept my apology and take my suggestion to visit a local library with a sufficient science section, or do a dive deep on the internet to research radioactive decay.) The YECs have failed in trying to make an issue of this. There are actually several more techniques available for dating material and separating the parent and daughter products. Your local library should contain some books on this subject and you will also find more recommended solutions concerning this problem on the internet. The YECs can go nowhere with this subject.

Explaining Antarctica's and Greenland's Ice Shelfs and the Ice Ages

It is well-known that both the Antarctic continent and the large island of Greenland are covered by huge and very thick sheets of ice. It is believed that these ice sheets are remnants of the global ice age that encapsulated the earth beginning several millions of years ago. These "ice caps" provide proof of an old earth, despite the claims of the YECs.

About forty years ago, when there was no such thing as satellite phones, I had the opportunity to serve my country by using my advanced-class amateur radio license[8] to relay phone traffic from the South Pole Station and McMurdo Sound Station in Antarctica up to our home in the USA. At the time, I was a young electrical engineer with dual radio licenses, a commercial and an amateur license. I was a United States Air Force veteran from the Vietnam era who enjoyed the fact that I could still be a help to my country. In those days, scientists and military personnel worked at the science stations in Antarctica collecting data on weather, astronomy, and some other, confidential things that I have sworn not to disclose. I enjoyed placing phone calls over my extensive radio station that allowed these scientific personnel in the Antarctic to talk to their loved ones back home in the States most every weekend. There were times when I spent eight to ten hours on Saturdays patching the radio phone calls stateside.

During my time of service to the Antarctic crew, I learned many things. First, I learned that the ice at the South Pole station was about nine thousand feet thick. Next I learned that the ice was made up of very small layers or increments of ice accumulated over thousands of years. Each layer represents the snowfall between the summer and winter seasons at the South Pole, and each layer varies slightly in thickness but averages about one-eighth to one-quarter of an inch thick per year. There is very little snow accumulation on these ice sheets for any particular year because the very low temperatures at the pole result in very little annual precipitation, so the growth is considerably slowed, much lower than the snowfall you may experience in your driveway. Despite the small amount of snow accumulation each year on the ice caps, there is a distinct layer left in the ice for each year because of the effects of the Antarctic winter and summer weather. By drilling down through the ice sheet, it is possible to collect a good record of the age of the ice sheet and to determine the type of weather experienced worldwide when each layer was laid down. Many labs around the nation have these ice cores refrigerated, and there are photographs of many for public viewing. One can also see pictures of these ice cores on the internet. The annual layers are rather distinct.

The National Oceanographic and Atmospheric Administration (NOAA) reports that the Antarctic ice sheets contain a record of hundreds of thousands of years of past world climate, completely trapped in the ancient snow layers. Scientists recover this climate history by drilling cores in the ice, some of them over thirty-five hundred meters (eleven thousand feet) deep.[9] Paleoclimate data has also shown that glacial cycles, a pattern of ice ages and glacial retreats lasting thousands of years, dominated the climate for the past two million years. During the peak of the most recent glacial cycle, about twenty-one thousand years ago, massive terrestrial ice sheets extended over large parts of North America and Europe, and global temperature was about 9°F colder than it is today.[10]

To pry climate clues out of the ice, scientists began to drill long cores out of the ice sheets in Greenland and Antarctica in the late 1960s. By the time that the Greenland Ice Sheet Project (GISP2 project) finished in the early 1990s, they had pulled a nearly two-mile-long core (3,053.44 meters) from the Greenland ice sheet, providing a record of at least the past 110,000 years. Even older records going back about 750,000 years have come out of Antarctica. For anyone who may be interested in the continental glaciers that once covered most of the Northern Hemisphere of the earth, I would suggest visiting many archeological museums around the nation, as I have done, to look at the vast amount of evidence. Afterward, try to suggest to a YEC that perhaps his or her opinions need to be reevaluated.

Geological Evidence of an Old Earth

There is a tremendous amount of data in the study of the earth's structure that suggests an old age of creation. Most high school or college textbooks on earth science or geology can answer most of your questions about the true age of the earth. One of the fascinating pieces of evidence that added proof for the age of the earth was discovered by US submarines cruising the Atlantic Ocean during World War II. While cruising the ocean searching for German submarines using the new tool called "sonar," the American subs continually discovered a tall rocky ridge along the center line of the Atlantic Ocean floor. Later, using cameras, it was discovered that this ridge was a crack in the earth's crust and that magma was being pushed up into the sea from this crack. The following information is taken from a 2011 report by the US Geological Survey:

> The Mid-Atlantic Ridge (MAR) is a mid-ocean ridge, a
> divergent tectonic plate boundary located along the floor

of the Atlantic Ocean, and is part of the longest mountain range in the world. In the North Atlantic it separates the Eurasian and North American Plates, and in the South Atlantic it separates the African and South American Plates. The ridge extends from a junction with the Mid-Arctic Ridge northeast from Greenland, southward to a Junction in the South Atlantic. Although the Mid-Atlantic Ridge is mostly an underwater feature, portions of it have enough elevation to extend above sea level. The section of the ridge that includes the island of Iceland is also known as the Reykjanes Ridge. The ridge has an average spreading rate of about 2.5 centimeters (0.98 in) per year.[11]

Based on the findings of the geological surveys, we now know that the earth's crust is made up of moving plates of stone that float atop the sea of magma in the earth. The magma is a sea of molten, red hot stone that lies under the earth's crust. The earth's crust is what makes up the continental shelves, and when these plates move, we suffer the phenomenon known as an earthquake.

What do we know for certain? We know that the North American continent is moving away from the European continent at the rate of about one inch per year. This figure has been confirmed by GPS measurements. We also know that the distance between New York and London is 3,465 miles. Therefore, with a scientific calculator we arrive at the conclusion that it took the North American continent about 219,542,400 years (approximately 220 million years) to move away from the European continent. Now I agree that this calculation may be off a bit, but it clearly demonstrates the vast amount of time needed for the continents to separate as far as they have. If you carefully examine a global map of the Atlantic, you can see that the European and African plates mesh closely with the North American and South American plates, respectively. This idea was fermented several centuries ago when the European explorers started making maps of their discoveries.

Quoting from a geology textbook, "Plate motion of lithospheric plates move very slowly—usually between 1 to 10 centimeters per year."[12] Another example of geological plate motion is the Great Rift Valley in

East Africa that ranges from northern Lebanon south as far as the Congo in Africa. This valley was created by a split in the earth's crust. Based on the velocity measurements thus far, geologists estimate that in less than one million years, East Africa will split off and form a new continent. In the meantime, hot magma is being pushed up from the earth's crack, and there is a series of live volcanos along the valley. The evidence is overwhelming and the information is readily available for all to see, but the YECs will argue that God made the continental plates separate quickly, in a short amount of time, during Noah's flood. Of course they have no proof, but they will suggest that if you refuse to believe their argument, then you are a "Christian atheist."

Fossils and Michigan's Petoskey Stone

I've been a resident of Michigan most of my life. I like to say that I live in the "Mitten State." It has been said that all Michiganders carry a map of Michigan in their right hip pockets. Just ask a person from Michigan where they live in the state and they will pull out the map with their right hand and point to a spot on their hand. Michigan has a lot of features that bring tourists every summer to the Great Lakes State with its hundreds of miles of clear blue water beaches and great fishing.

However, Michigan has another special feature that amazes the tourists, and that is the state "stone" (declared by the legislature in 1965). This special stone was first discovered in the upper half of Michigan's Lower Peninsula many years ago (perhaps the local Indians found them first). You can find these stones in almost all of the many gift shops in northern Michigan, which like to charge too much for them, but if you scour the sandy beaches you can pick some up for free. "What are these stones?" you ask. They are called Petoskey stones, because these stones were first found in the sides of the cliffs along the shore of Lake Michigan near Petoskey. These cliffs are loaded with fossil remnants imbedded in the rocks found along the shoreline and in the cliffs, some as tall as two hundred feet. Now if you ever have an opportunity to visit, I can't recommend enough that you should also visit the beautiful cities along the northern shoreline of the state, surrounded by the sky-blue waters of Lake Michigan.

When you stop by, pick up a Petoskey stone at a Michigan gift shop, and there you will clearly see a piece of fossilized coral reef. When you find one of these stones on the beach, you will need to sand smooth one side of it and then polish the sanded side until it is shiny and clear enough to see the fine detail of the coral formation. These stones are so beautiful when polished that, for many years, the local Indians made jewelry with them. You can pick up some of the Indian artwork samples at the local gift shops.

Let's get technical for a moment: geologists have determined that the state of Michigan and the surrounding area is sitting on top of a very ancient coral reef. According to the Bible, the earth, in the beginning, was entirely covered with water (Genesis 1:2; Psalm 104:5,6). That agrees with the findings of the geologists, because ancient fossilized beds of coral reefs have been found all over the earth. Coral fossils like the Petoskey stones have been found in Iowa, Indiana, Illinois, Ohio, and New York; locations in Canada, Germany, and England; and even some places in Asia.

In today's world, we find coral reefs mostly in the warm tropics where the coral can grow and multiply. A coral reef is made up of vast numbers of small structures or shells, each one being the shell housing of a coral, which is a very small invertebrate creature that lives in a calcium carbonate shell. These shells are built one upon another as time allows, and the layers of these shells become what is known as a coral reef. The shells look like miniature seashells when examined up close.

During World War II, many of our marines fought on islands in the Pacific Ocean that were formed from coral reefs, such as Enewetak and Kwajalein Islands. These islands were built up of coral over many centuries. A quote from our geology book states, "Coral reefs are built very slowly over thousands of years."[13] In time, the creatures that built the reef die off, but the reef remains and serves a valuable function for the ocean, as the reef can become home for much of the sea life. The reef also can act as an erosion barrier protecting the shoreline, such as the Great Barrier Reef of eastern Australia does now.

Now the Petoskey stones are fossil remnants of ancient coral reefs from about four hundred million years ago, during the Devonian period. During this time, most of the earth was covered by water in which sea life abounded. When you closely examine the stones, you clearly see the shape and size of each coral shell embedded in the stone, but you also see the very clear stone that covers the shell, and that stone is quartz. The coral shells are packed tightly together in clear, transparent quartz. The only way this could happen is if the coral reef were tightly packed in an environment rich in silicon dioxide (quartz, SiO_2—common sand), where the silicon dioxide mineral could replace the calcium carbonate (calcite, $CaCO_3$) shell through a process similar to osmosis. The result of this process is called "silification."[14] This is the means whereby each crystal of silicon dioxide can replace a molecule of calcium carbonate. The result is a very stable stone at the earth's surface. As the miniature coral creatures die off, the resulting shells undergo the silification process and are flawlessly kept embedded in the quartz stone. In time, this quartz sinks into the earth and is heated, creating the clear, transparent stone. This layer of quartz stone may rise to the surface because of geological plate uplift (as is the case in Petoskey, Michigan). Many people collect and polish these fossils to make jewelry and ornaments from them. It is also claimed that some of these fossil remains were broken off from the bedrock underlying northern Michigan by the glaciers that once covered the northern states. The sad news for the YECs is that these coral reefs can take hundreds of thousands of years to form, so they were not formed during the supposed world-wide flood with Noah. They are formed over thousands of years and then fossilized by being kept in stone for millions of years, until the earth releases them through continental plate shifts and uplifts. (If anyone would like to purchase one of these stones for an ornament, please visit Petoskey, Michigan, a beautiful city on the shores of northern Lake Michigan.)

The purpose of this chapter is not to present an in-depth analysis of each of the scientific methods mentioned. If the reader should desire to know more of the details, then he or she only need visit a public library, go to a university bookstore, or do an in-depth search on the internet. As I stated before, the purpose of this chapter is to point to specific well known data that clearly demonstrate the age of God's creation. In this chapter, I have explained in detail seven items that show the earth and all creation were created by God a very long time ago, much longer than is claimed by the young earth creationists. If only one of my arguments is true, then I have shown that the universe is very old—like about 13.76 billion years old.

Next we need to study the nature of the ancient civilizations that lived in the middle east about the time Moses wrote the first book of the Bible.

[1] David R. Montgomery, *The Rocks Don't Lie* (New York: W. W. Norton, 2012), 256.

[2] Brian Cox and J. Forshaw, *Why Does E=mc²?* (Cambridge, MA: Da Capo Press, 2009), 30–32.

[3] *The Astrophysical Journal* 688 (November 20, 2008): L21–L24.

[4] E. M. Henley and A. Garcia, *Subatomic Physics*, 3rd ed. (Hackensack: World Scientific Publishing, 2007), 299.

[5] David Halliday, R. Resnick, and J. Walker, *Fundamentals of Physics*, 7th ed. (Hoboken: J. Wiley & Sons, 2005), 892.

[6] Nancy Forbes and B. Mahon, *Faraday, Maxwell, and the Electromagnetic Field* (Amherst, NY: Prometheus Books, 2014), 217.

[7] Some items on this subject were taken from an article found online called "Radiometric Dating: A Christian Perspective," by Dr. Roger C. Wiens (2002); however, most of the text is from my own studies and background.

[8] My license first issued in 1968 and still current is WA8WAA.

[9] Holli Riebeek, "Paleoclimatology: The Ice Core Record," NASA Earth Observatory, December 19, 2005, https://earthobservatory.nasa.gov/Features/Paleoclimatology_IceCores/.

[10] www.ncdc.noaa.gov/news/what-have-we-learned-paleoclimatology.

[11] "Understanding Plate Motions," United States Geological Survey, last updated September 14, 2015, https://pubs.usgs.gov/gip/dynamic/understanding.html.

[12] Barbara Murck, *Geology: A Self Teaching Guide* (New York: John Wiley & Sons, 2001), 18.

[13] Murck, 210.

[14] http://en.citizendium.org wiki/Fossilization/palaeontology.

CHAPTER 7

An Examination of Ancient Cosmologies

The Bible has a message for all times, but it comes dressed in a unique cultural setting. If one desires to grasp the biblical meaning fully, one must seek to understand the culture of those ancient times wherein the Bible was written. This presents a danger to our modern evangelical churches when we read scripture, not as it was intended, but as a message exclusively for our time and culture. Simply stated, the world of the Bible is not our world.

We read in Exodus that God commissioned Moses to lead the children of Israel out of the land of Egypt. It appeared to be God's purpose to free the people of Israel from slavery in Egypt and lead them to another land, where He would establish His reign over a holy kingdom. However, the children of Israel had lived in Egypt for about four hundred years, and they were in need of an education about the real and only God, the God of their father Abraham. I believe that the purpose of the forty years of wandering in the deserts of Arabia was to prepare the people in their understanding of the only true God and to build a kingdom of God in the land of Canaan. One could say that the forty years of wandering in the desert was their seminary or Bible college so that in the end they would truly know their God, the God of Gods, the Almighty God, the only God, the Creator God.

When archeologists examined the writings of the ancients, one of the conclusions they came to was that the ancients really did not concern themselves with where everything came from. Every ancient civilization developed its own ideas about the creation of the land, the sky, the sea, animals, and humankind. The science of creation was not part of their reasoning; their major concern was the theology of creation. Reading the fables passed down from the ancients, one can see a mixture of serious attempts to explain everything and make-believe.

One common phenomenon among ancient religions was the belief that everything, for example, trees, mountains, sky, clouds, animals, stars, and rocks, was possessed by spirits. All spirits were considered gods, some greater than others. The ancients' gods were defined as anyone and anything, spirit or human, that was immortal and all-wise. This was the culture that the Hebrew children dwelt in during their years of captivity in Egypt. When we study the first five books of the Bible, we needs to remember that the ancient Egyptian religion was the major religious influence on the Hebrew slaves and all who lived in Egypt. The common religion of that day was a complex system of polytheistic beliefs and rituals that were an essential part of the ancient Egyptian society.

Prior to the advent of Christianity, the Egyptians interacted with many gods who were believed to be present in, and in control of, the forces of nature. Prayers and offerings were made to provide for the gods and gain their favor. All formal religious practice was focused on the pharaoh, the king of Egypt, who was believed to be a god and to possess divine powers. He acted as the intermediary, a high priest between his people and the gods, and was obligated to sustain the gods through rituals and offerings so that they would maintain order in the cosmos. The pharaoh dedicated enormous resources to Egyptian rituals and to the construction of numerous temples.

Figure 7.1[1] illustrates the ancient Egyptian view of the cosmos. This picture clearly shows the ancient Egyptian obsession with the supernatural world. Shown in figure 7.1 is a short list of some of the common gods of ancient Egypt. It has been estimated that the ancient Egyptians worshipped upwards of two thousand gods. Notice that the god Nut holds up the sky, confirming the popular and false concept of a "firmament," as explained in chapter 8 of *And There Was Light* and as mentioned in Genesis 1:14 (KJV). The Hebrew word used here is *raqia* (pronounced "ra-kee-a"), which the *New American Standard Bible* translates as "expanse" instead of "firmament" as in the KJV Bible.

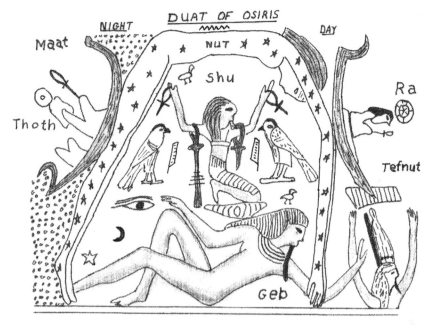

FIGURE 7.1 DUAT OF OSIRIS

Some of the most widely worshipped gods in the Egyptian religion were Osiris, god of the underworld; Isis, the goddess of motherhood and abundance; Horus, god of the sky (and son of Osiris and Isis); Anubis, the funerary god; Ra, the sun god; Nut the goddess of the sky; and Seth, the god of chaos and destruction. Some villages chose a specific god to represent them, whereas some individuals chose a god that supported their profession, such as Thoth, the god of scribes. Many gods were also represented by animals, such as cats, crocodiles, rams, buffalo, frogs, jackals and lions.

The pharaoh was seen as an intermediary between the gods and humans, that is, sort of a priest, and he was believed to be part god, part man. If things were going well, it was because the pharaoh was maintaining good relations with the gods. One of Egypt's most famous pharaohs was Akhenaten, who abandoned the worship of other gods and headed the only monotheistic period in ancient Egypt with his worship of the sun-disk Aten, the "sun god."

Ancient Egyptians believed in an afterlife, which was a commonly held belief among many peoples, and they created special rituals for death and burial to prepare a dead loved one for the afterlife. The rituals included the process of mummifying the body in order to maintain its original condition. They believed that after death, the spirit of the deceased could continue to dwell in the mummified body. The body, which was covered with amulets and jewels, was wrapped in cloth, and a mask bearing the person's likeness in life was placed over the face. Depending on the person's status, food, drink, and riches were also stored in the tomb for use in the next life.

Worship and ritual affected every aspect of Egyptian life. The ancient Greek historian Herodotus said of the Egyptians that they were "religious to a higher degree than any other people." They built an extraordinary number of temples for the purposes of daily worship and ritual, as well as for elaborate religious ceremonies and festivals. Luxor Temple and Karnak are among the most impressive and the most visited today. However, ancient Egypt is most famous for its pyramids, the great tombs built by the pharaohs to house their remains. The largest is the Great Pyramid of Khufu, considered one of the Seven Wonders of the Ancient World. It must be considered that after four hundred years of living in Egypt, most or many of the Hebrews became adherents to the Egyptian religions.

Because the Greeks were the leading thinkers of their day, in time their ideas became accepted by many other cultures. The Greeks believed in many gods, and if you asked them where their gods came from, they would reply that the Titans created them. Then if you asked the Greeks where the Titans came from, they would reply that they have no idea. In the eternal universe of Aristotle, the earth was perfectly at rest. The Greeks assumed that the land on which they dwelt and the sky with all it contained were eternal, without beginning or end. The cosmos (world), if it ever had any transitional motion, would have eventually come to rest in the center of all creation, its natural place. Further, the Greeks believed that the cosmos could not be spinning on an axis because circular motion was only appropriate for the more perfect heavens, not for the imperfect entities of the sub-lunar region.

They believed that the sun, the moon, and the planets all maintained the same distance from the land (or earth) at all times. Because the stars were all attached to the celestial sphere (the "firmament," translated "expanse" in the *NASB*), they maintained the same distance from the earth and the same relationship to one another at all times.[2] The ancient Greeks (as well as the people of most other ancient civilizations) understood that the earth (world) was flat and surrounded by an ocean that circled it. Further, they believed that if one sailed far enough out into the ocean, one would fall off the world and land up in the abyss.

I must remind the reader that among the ancient civilizations (at least until the sixteenth century), the belief in a flat world was totally common. Therefore, we find while reading the Bible that there is no correction given for this lack of understanding of our physical world. The truth simply is that God was not trying to teach the Hebrew children about the physics of creation, but instead a God-centered philosophy of creation. Figure 7.2 is an example of the ancient understanding of earth. This is the oldest known example of humankind's understanding of the shape of the earth. Figure 7.2 illustrates this commonly held view of the world. I would like to add that there is nothing in the Bible that contradicts the view of a flat earth. The Bible is not a book on world geography. Instead, the Bible is a book on humankind's relationship with the eternal Creator, the Lord God Almighty. In His revelation to humankind, God had to accommodate humankind's ignorance of the physical universe.

I have included a map of the known world in chapter 5 (figure 5.1). Please refer to it again for this discussion. This map is based on the teaching of the first recognized historian, Herodotus, a Greek scholar of the fifth century BC (estimated to have lived sometime around 450 BC). In common with the beliefs of most ancient nations, the Hebrews' belief was that the earth was not only the central point of the universe but also the central point of the universe itself, with every other body, the heavens, the sun, the moon, and the stars being subsidiary to and, as it were, the complement of the earth. The Hebrew language has no expression equivalent to denote our universe, except the phrase "the heavens and the earth." With regard to the earth's body, the Hebrews conceived its surface to be an immense flat disc, supported like the flat roof of an Eastern house, by pillars (Job 9:6; Psalm 75:3) that rested on solid foundations (Job 38:4,6; Psalm 104:5; Proverbs 8:29).[3]

When you read the Old Testament, you must understand that this illustration represents what the ancient people thought of when someone mentioned "the heavens and earth." They had no other idea to rely on.

From a cosmological point of view, the popular conception of the world, or cosmos, was that illustrated in figure 7.2.[4]

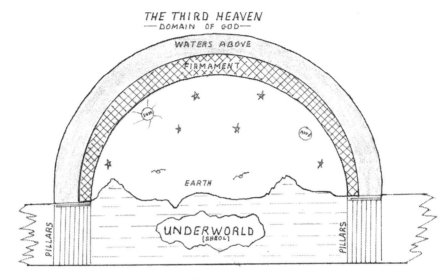

FIGURE 7.2 CHART OF THE COSMOS

The earth was flat and it was surrounded by the sky. The sun, moon, and stars were held in place by the sky, and it was the sky that traveled across the heavens. Above the sky was the "firmament," which held back the waters of heaven, and above that was the abode of God. Beneath the earth was the underworld, also known as the abyss, where the dead dwelt until the coming resurrection in the last days.

The apostle Paul testifies to the accuracy of this depiction in 2 Corinthians 12:1–4, where he writes the following:

> Boasting is necessary, though it is not profitable; but I will go on to visions and revelations of the Lord. I know a man in Christ who fourteen years ago—whether in the body I do not know, or out of the body I do not know, God knows—such a man was *caught up to the third heaven* (the heaven of heavens). And I know how such a man—whether in the body or apart from the body I do not know, God knows—was caught up into Paradise and

heard inexpressible words, which a man is not permitted
to speak. (emphasis added)

Paul was explaining to the Corinthian church his calling to the
ministry by the Lord. He wrote that he was taken up to the third heaven.
The third heaven is the domain of God, as illustrated in figure 7.2.
According to the ancients, the second heaven was the domain of the sun,
moon, and stars, and the first heaven was where the birds flew and clouds
lay. If you had told one of the ancients that the earth was a giant round
ball that was flying around the sun at 66,700 miles per hour, he would
have thought you were crazy and possessed by evil spirits. The ancient
languages, including Hebrew, had no word for "planet" or "universe."
They didn't need such a word. Stop for a moment and think how God
should have led Moses to write the creation story in the first two chapters
of Genesis. How would you have written the story so that it would be
scientifically correct and at the same time understandable to the ancients
thirty-four hundred years ago?

Can you see the problem? I am certain that the overriding purpose
of Genesis 1–11 was to dispel the ancient myths that the Hebrew people
had learned while they lived in Egypt for four hundred years. Egypt was a
pagan country whose people believed that the pharaoh was a god and the
sun was the all-powerful god. Then there were many other gods whom
the people worshipped. As an example, there were gods of the harvest,
gods of the city, gods of the tribes, gods of the sea, and gods of the Nile
River. Do you see God's purpose in the first books of the Bible? It was to
teach the sons of Abraham, Isaac, and Jacob that the Lord Jehovah was
the only true God and that there were no other gods.

Remember, Moses recorded God's proclamation to Abraham in
Genesis 17:1 that He is the Almighty God [El-Shaddai, the first time this
term is used in the Bible] and there is none other. The Hebrew children
perhaps had never heard of this before. Remember, they were in captivity
about four hundred years, and Abraham lived somewhere around 2000
BC, and between four hundred and six hundred years before the Exodus.
It was God's purpose to create a people and a kingdom for Himself from
this rabble that He rescued from bondage in Egypt. So when you read
Genesis, remember this truth: God wrote it for the Hebrew people, and

now thirty-four hundred years later we can benefit by learning the true nature and purpose of the real God and apply these truths to our own lives as we seek to worship Him and serve Him. But we would be very foolish to adjust our understanding of the nature of the universe to the beliefs of early humankind.

[1] This illustration was found on the internet with no source indicated; therefore no approval could be received. It is considered as part of the public domain because it is an ancient illustration.

[2] L. M. Dolling et al., eds., *The Tests of Time* (Princeton, NJ: Princeton University Press, 2003), 5.

[3] John McClintock and James Strong, *Cyclopedia of Biblical, Theological, and Ecclesiastical Literature*, vol. 2. (Grand Rapids, MI: Baker Book House, 1981), 526, 528.

[4] This illustration was found on the internet with no source indicated; therefore, no approval could be received. It is considered as part of the public domain because it is an ancient illustration.

CHAPTER 8

The First Chapters of Genesis

Roger Penrose and I showed that Einstein's general theory of relativity implied that the universe must have had a beginning, and possibly an end.

—Stephen Hawking (noted atheist)[1]

The outstanding feature of Genesis 1–11 is a polemic against the pagan cosmologies of its day. It speaks of the one and only true God, Jehovah (יהוה), the God of Abraham, Isaac, and Jacob. As author, God refuted the common pagan belief that there were many gods and taught the Hebrew people, through the writings of Moses, that there was only one true Creator God. Therefore, it was necessary to explain the idea of creation from His perspective and in such a manner that the readers could correctly understand it. To fulfill this purpose, God left out many of the physical details of the creation and explained it in a simple way that the average fifteenth-century BC Hebrew peasant could understand. Remember, God was not communicating the creation narrative to twenty-first-century science scholars. And if He had, I'm confident that we would not have been able to understand Him. Therefore, in all His communications, it was necessary for God to accommodate our intellectual weakness.

My purpose in this chapter is not to completely exegete the first eleven chapters of Genesis, but instead to show that the literal English translation and reading can sometimes lead to a complete misunderstanding of the message contained therein. Those who have fixed their minds on the dismissal of the facts of proven scientific inquiry need to rethink their positions, because otherwise they risk making biblical Christianity the laughingstock of the educated masses. As I have mentioned before, I hold to the inerrancy of Holy Scripture in all that it affirms, but not in what it communicates concerning ancient Near Eastern presuppositions about the natural world and universe. I clearly see that God had to accommodate the ancients so that they might believe Him. This is not implying that God is deceitful; instead, it is saying that He is flexible and can make adjustments in the process of communication.

Let's begin with the first several verses in the Bible: "In the beginning God created the heavens and the earth. The earth was formless and void, and darkness was over the surface of the deep, and the Spirit of God was moving over the surface of the waters. Then God said, 'Let there be light'; and there was light" (Genesis 1:1–3).

The first verse in the Hebrew Old Testament is thus;

בְּרֵאשִׁית בָּרָא אֱלֹהִים אֵת הַשָּׁמַיִם וְאֵת הָאָרֶץ : (Genesis 1:1).

The first word of the Bible as given above, *barashith* (בְּרֵאשִׁית),[2] is literally translated as "in a beginning," because there is no definite article such as *the* before the word "beginning". Notice that Hebrew is read right to left. The phrase "in the beginning" is an incorrect translation. Without the article, the verse could be translated as, "In a beginning God created the heavens and the earth." However, this first word in Hebrew is translated in the Jewish translations as "When God began" or "While God began." The reason for this translation is simply that the grammar shows that the first sentence in our traditional English translation is actually a clause that is part of a longer sentence, or as referred to by the grammarians, part of a Hebrew construct, a prepositional phrase that introduces the following subject of creation. The Hebrew preposition בּ *bath,* which is attached to the beginning of the Hebrew word, can be translated as "in, on, by, with, within, among." These are just a few examples taken from the *Classical Hebrew Lexicon* by Brown, Driver, and Briggs.

The following is an example of the current Jewish translation of the first verse of Genesis: "When God began to create heaven and earth—the earth being unformed and void, with darkness over the surface of the deep and a wind from God sweeping over the water—God said, 'Let there be light.'"[3]

Another example of a Jewish translation is given as, "In the beginning of God's creating the skies and the earth—when the earth had been shapeless and formless and darkness was on the face of the deep, and God's spirit was hovering on the face of the water—God said, 'Let there be light.'"[4]

These translations place the verb *to be* (יְהִי), in the main clause, which is in verse 3, and that is where God revealed light. God said, "Let there be light", where <u>let there be</u> is the verb meaning "to be, to be done", it is a verb which is in the imperfect tense, third person singular, and masculine. The first three verses in Genesis 1 are one sentence made up of three clauses, and the principle verb is in the third clause.

The missing definite article in the first Hebrew word in the Old Testament makes verse 1 a clause appearing before the main sentence containing the principal verb as described above. The fact of the missing definite article is confirmed by a further Hebrew Old Testament known as the Septuagint, a Greek translation produced sometime between 150 and 200 BC by Jewish scholars in order to reach Greek-speaking Jews of the Alexandrian empire, the largest empire in the world at that time.

The first sentence in the Greek Old Testament (LXX, a.k.a. the Septuagint) reads as ἐν ἀρχῇ ἐποίησεν ὁ θεὸς τὸν οὐρανὸν καὶ τὴν γῆν, and it translates as, "In beginning God made the heavens and the earth." Again we notice that there is no definite article *the* before the word ἀρχῇ (i.e., "beginning"), but there is a definite article before each of the words *heaven* and *earth*. This Greek translation created by Hebrew scholars more than two thousand years ago confirms that the original Hebrew text created about thirty-five hundred years ago did not have the definite article before the word for *beginning*, thereby confirming that the first verse is actually a prepositional phrase, followed by the main clause in verse 3.

Let me add that there is further confirmation in the Greek New Testament, in the first verse of the Gospel of John, where we read, "Ἐν ἀρχῇ ἦν ὁ λόγος," which literally translates as, "In beginning was the Word." Again we see that the definite article *the* before the word *beginning* is missing, confirming the ancient version of the Septuagint (from which this verse was copied and adapted to the person of Christ by the apostle John), and confirming the ancient Hebrew of Genesis 1. Therefore each of these translators was copying the first verse of Genesis correctly, and the currently accepted Jewish interpretation appears to be correct; that is, "Let there be light" is the main part of the first sentence in scripture and the principal verb in that sentence.

Returning to Genesis 1, the actual first word, without the preposition ב meaning "in," is *rashith* (רֵאשִׁית) (*Strongest* #7221). This word is most often translated in English as "beginning." Well-known Hebrew scholar Dr. John Sailhamer, in his book *Genesis Unbound*, provides a translation of the word *beginning* in relation to its temporal meaning. He writes as follows:

> The Hebrew word *rashith*, which is the term for "beginning" ... has a very specific sense in Scripture. In the Bible, *the term always refers to an extended, yet indeterminate duration of time*—not a specific moment. It is a block of time which precedes an extended series of time periods ... The term does not refer to a point in time but to a period or duration of time which falls before a series of events.[5] (emphasis added)

The *Zondervan Pictorial Encyclopedia of the Bible* adds this comment in its section on creation, referring to this subject: "It has to be recognized that as far as the Bible is concerned, the Old Testament account of creation does not preface the rest of scripture as though it were an isolated attempt in antiquity to explain the origins of phenomena and human life. Indeed, if the first word of Genesis, בְּרֵאשִׁית is translated correctly to read 'by way of beginning' or 'to begin with,' it will relate to something other than an absolute temporal start to creation. What the position of the creation narratives show, is that for the ancient Semitic writers creation was the starting point of history."[6]

In conclusion, translations of the creation narrative from the ancient Hebrew sources reveal that Genesis 1 does not necessarily support a recent creation theory; in fact, it can be read to contradict it. The word *beginning* is not a set onetime event, but rather a temporal process as explained in the many lexicons.

Next we need to examine the *natural divisions* in the book of Genesis. The chapter divisions that we now recognize were not part of the original text but were added many years after the original writing, some claim by the Masoretes (a sect of Jewish scribes of the seventh and eighth centuries AD, approximately). However, it has also been proposed that the current chapter divisions were the result of the work of Stephen Langton[7] (AD 1150–1228) in the Latin manuscripts of his day. Since these chapter divisions may have been added by Christian scholars during the Middle Ages, a more thorough understanding of Genesis might be had by following its natural division system, one based on Moses's literary cues (written two thousand years earlier), which he uses to emphasize the early fathers of the Hebrew people. Beginning with Adam and ending with Jacob (Israel), this division of Genesis is established by repeating the word *toledoth* before each section. Examine the following list of verses taken from the *NASB* version of the Old Testament (all emphasis is mine).

- Genesis 2:4: "This is the *account* [toledoth] of the heavens and the earth when they were created, in the day that the Lord God made earth and heaven."
- Genesis 5:1: "This is the book of the *generations* [toledoth] of Adam. In the day when God created man."
- Genesis 6:9: "These are the records of the *generations* [toledoth] of Noah."
- Genesis 10:1: "Now these are the records of the *generations* [toledoth] of Shem, Ham, and Japheth, the sons of Noah; and sons were born to them after the flood."
- Genesis 11:10: "These are the records of the *generations* [toledoth] of Shem."
- Genesis 11:27: "Now these are the records of the *generations* [toledoth] of Terah."
- Genesis 25:12: "Now these are the records of the *generations* [toledoth] of Ishmael, Abraham's son, whom Hagar the Egyptian, Sarah's maid, bore to Abraham."
- Genesis 25:19: "Now these are the records of the *generations* [toledoth] of Isaac, Abraham's son."

- Genesis 36:1: "Now these are the records of the *generations* [toledoth] of Esau (that is, Edom)."
- Genesis 36:9: "These then are the records of the *generations* [toledoth] of Esau the father of the Edomites in the hill country of Seir."
- Genesis 37:2: "These are the records of the *generations* [toledoth] of Jacob."

The Hebrew word *toledoth,* תּוֹלְדוֹת (*Strong's* #8435) can be translated as "account, births, genealogies, family line, records, generations, etc."

Now this list of scripture references was created to demonstrate that each time the author of Genesis used the word *toledoth,* it was to introduce a list of descendants or the results of some previous activity. Then it follows that Genesis 2:4 is referring to the results or descendants of the previous section. This stands to reason when we read in Genesis 2:5 that there were no shrubs or plants in the land and there was no man to till the ground. "Now no shrub of the field was yet in the earth, and no plant of the field had yet sprouted, for the Lord God had not sent rain upon the earth, and there was no man to cultivate the ground."

This is very confusing when we read in the first chapter, verses 11 and 12, that God had created the foliage (trees and plants) to cover the earth (on the third day) and then God created man on the sixth day. So from our vantage point it seems as if the Bible has a contradiction. I don't believe so. Instead, our problem is our failure to understand the actual meaning of the text.

We read that God created man and woman in Genesis 1:27 and again in Genesis 2:7. This presents an unusual problem. Were there two creations of humankind, or is verse 2:7 just a recapitulation of the first mention? You may spot a significant difference when you notice that only in verse 2:7 does God breathe into the man the "breath of life." He doesn't do this in verse 1:27. Is this significant? Possibly. Could it be that verse 1:27 is referring to the creation of an original man (a humanoid) and that verse 2:7 is referring specifically to Adam, a different man, one with God's breath in him? I don't believe that chapter 2 is referring to a second creation. We can't allow a contradiction in our interpretation of scripture, so we are forced to suggest that we just don't know everything and possibly never will. An important matter to consider is that *the Hebrew words for* man, men, *and also* Adam *are identical.* So with the Hebrew language, the original language of the Old Testament, it is not possible to determine if the word *man* refers to Adam or to a generic man. Context may provide the answer, but in some things we may not be able to distinguish the difference. We must begin with the assumption that God has not provided us with answers to all our questions.

Could the idea of mankind (or humankind) existing before Adam answer the problem created when Cain says that he is afraid someone will kill him (Genesis 4:14)? Based on the literal, common interpretation of the common English translation, there were only four people on earth at the time, Adam, Eve, Cain, and Abel. So who was Cain afraid of when he said, in Genesis 4:14, "Someone will kill me"? Who is this someone? Was it one of his brothers born of Adam and Eve and matured some fifteen to twenty years later? This doesn't make sense. Cain could have made himself impossible to find in the wilderness of this large earth so that no one would be able to locate him. As an example, he could have fled over the Himalayan Mountains into China. No one would be able to find him there. Cain's concern would be easy to understand if we assumed that the world that he knew about was limited to the area of Eden, or the southern Mesopotamian valley. Do you see how one's perspective changes when one sees things from an ancient viewpoint?

Later we read that Cain had a wife in Genesis 4:17. The question is, where did she come from? Did Cain have to wait for Adam and Eve to have a daughter and for her to mature fourteen to twenty years later so that he would have a sister to marry? This logic doesn't make sense. Then later in the verse we read that Cain built a city. Where did all the inhabitants come from? Did Cain have to wait while his parents had a daughter and raised her to adult age, and then did Cain have to wait while he and she had enough children to populate a small village or city? This does not make sense either. We must conclude that God had left out of the narrative much detail, and this fact arouses our curiosity.

Now let's ask ourselves this question: Could the idea of humankind before Adam answer the question as to where Cain's wife came from and who populated the city that he built (Genesis 4:17)? These are important questions often avoided by young earth creation (YEC) advocates. In other words, could Adam be a separate, later creation of God, made in His image, with the breath of God indwelling (Genesis 2:7), contrary to the living bipedal humanlike creatures of that time? Is there some evidence in the paleontology records? Yes, we have thousands of skeletal samples of Neanderthal man and other humanlike creatures in museums around the world, and the public is invited to view them in most cases. These remains date back many thousands of years, so the earth must be older than as calculated by Bishop Ussher.

This brings up the next subject, concerning the "days" of creation. Think for a moment: if you had to explain the whole creation narrative to peoples of the ancient Near East, would you, or could you, use phrases such as "billions of years"? What would you expect their response to be? Further, must we assume that the six days of creation are connected by time as an immediate sequence, or in other words, that there is no time lapse between these days? There is no reason to make this assumption. For example, we read in Genesis 28:10–11 about a trip Jacob made to Beersheba where there is no mention of time, yet we know he had to have traveled about sixty miles, and a trip over the mountains of Canaan could have easily taken four to five days. It did not happen immediately, yet the author saw no need to include time in the discourse. Why would a YEC insist that each day described in Genesis would have to be in an immediate sequence, with no time gap between any of the days? There is no logical reason for such an assumption.

Let's look at what some of our most respective theologians have said concerning this issue. Respecting the length of the six days of creation, speaking generally, for there was some difference of views, the patristic and medieval exegesis makes the time out to be long periods, not days of twenty-four hours. The later interpretation has prevailed only in the modern church. Augustine teaches (in *De Genesi ad literam*, IV, xxvii) that the length of the six days is not to be determined by the length of our weekdays.[8] Augustine introduced a novelty into the way of approaching the biblical record of creation, an allegorical or nonliteral interpretation of Genesis 1. This method resulted in a view that the six days of creation were not literal days but was a device to show the progressive knowledge of creation.[9]

There is no reason to assume that a miracle must happen suddenly and not over a long period of time. God created all, but the question still lingers, how long did He take to do it? The truth is, we just don't know, because He chose not to tell us. Remember, time is the result of creation. Time is an attribute of space, and space is the result of creation. Anyone familiar with general relativity knows that time and space are inseparable. Therefore the use of the word *day* could very well be God's way of sequencing the miraculous creation phenomenon.

> "There is nothing in the use of the word 'day,' by Moses, that requires it to be explained as invariably denoting a period of 24 hours; but much to forbid it."[10]

> "Scripture contains data which oblige us to think of these days of Genesis as different from our ordinary units as determined by the revolutions of the earth."[11]

A simple point that Dr. Herman Bavinck (1854-1921) made in his book *Our Reasonable Faith* is that day and night on the other side of the world would be the opposite of that sequence for Moses and his people. Remember, Moses and the Hebrews believed that the world was flat, so that fact alone solved their problem concerning "days." "Morning" to Moses was morning everywhere in the world, all at the same time. This could only be true if the earth was flat and the sun rotated around the earth. Gleason L. Archer in his *Survey of the Old Testament* writes, "Nevertheless, on the basis of internal evidence, it is the writers conviction that *yom* (Hebrew word for day) in Genesis One could not have been intended by the Hebrew author to mean a literal twenty-four-hour day."[12]

Likewise, Millard J. Erickson writes in his *Theology Text*, "The *day-age theory* fits quite well with the geological record, especially if one sees some topical grouping as well."[13] The day-age theory was proposed many years ago as a possible solution to the question about the length of the days in Genesis 1. Some suggested that each day in the creation narrative was actually a long time of indeterminate length. This theory would allow for the known geological data showing an old earth and at the same time allow for the biblical narrative of "day" to be accepted as correct when understood as a metaphor.

Notice, God refers to the light as "day" and the darkness as "night." There is no mention of night or day on the other side of the globe (our earth), which obviously would be opposite that on the side on which Moses stood. This clearly demonstrates that God was leading Moses to write the account of creation according to the common perception of that time: that is, the earth (world) was flat and stationary and the sun and the heavens revolved around the earth. God did not intend to give the children of Israel a science lesson, so He left them all in their ignorance of astronomy. This is called "accommodation," and this is exactly what God did, knowing that any attempt to try to teach the Hebrew children the principles of physics and astronomy would take too much time and cost too much space on the written scrolls—and they wouldn't understand it anyway. God's purpose was to tell the Hebrews that He, the Almighty, the Eternal Creator and only God, was responsible for all creation and there were no other gods but Him.

It is important to insert a comment about what our Bible says concerning the length of days from God's viewpoint. In Psalm 90:4 we read, "For a thousand years in Your sight are like yesterday when it passes by, Or as a watch in the night."

And again in 2 Peter 3:8, we read, "But do not let this one fact escape your notice, beloved, that with the Lord one day is like a thousand years, and a thousand years like one day."

It is clear from these two verses that the Bible does not always equate the word *day* to a fixed period of time, such as twelve hours or twenty-four hours. I have given numerous examples of this truth in *And There Was Light* thus far, and I will be adding even more in later chapters. Now let's look at what a well-known and trusted theologian, Louis Berkhof (1873-1957), thinks: "The days referred to are God's days, the archetypal days, of which the days of men are merely ectypal copies; and with God a thousand years are as a single day (Psa. 90:4, 2 Pet 3:8). God has no days, but dwells in eternity, exalted above all measurements of time."[14]

Now some interpret these passages as being merely representative of God's view concerning the fulfillment of His prophecies, having nothing to do with "time" as God considers it. That is the view of the YECs. At this point, let me suggest that God is eternal and that time is a result of creation; therefore, humankind lives in the realm of time, but God does not. The Bible supports this conclusion that God is timeless in the following verses:

- "Before the mountains were born or You gave birth to the earth and the world, Even from everlasting to everlasting, You are God" (Psalm 90:2).
- "Who alone possesses immortality and dwells in unapproachable light, whom no man has seen or can see. To Him be honor and eternal dominion! Amen" (1 Timothy 6:16).

Let's be sure to understand what these two verses say. Simply stated, these verses declare that God's time and timing is not the same as humankind's. Therefore we are faced with this fact concerning the use of the word *day* in the first chapter of Genesis. For some, the Bible seems to state that God made everything in six connected twenty-four-hour days, and then He rested on the seventh day. In addition, many claim that the creation was completed just a little over six thousand years ago, based on the genealogical tables in the Bible, assuming for instance that there are no gaps in the genealogical lists (both of these are faulty assumptions). In Chapter 5 of this book we have explained this issue of God's timing rather completely and request that the reader go back to chapter 5 for a review.

The reason that the YECs are adamant in their denial of an old earth (or universe) is simply because they believe in evolution. By this statement I am saying that the YECs believe that if the universe is billions of years old, then evolution must be true. However, logically one idea does not naturally follow the other. An old earth concept does not require that life as we know it must have been formed by an unintelligent accident commonly called "evolution." The answer I always give to those who inquire about this matter is that we just don't know, and possibly never will. Regardless of the age of the universe, I cannot accept any other conclusion about creation except to say that God did it. I believe that when the universe began, God fully orchestrated the creation of everything according to His timing and His methods, even if it was billions of years ago.

Since we know that God is eternal, without beginning or end, may

I suggest that God does not dwell in our time domain? That is exactly what God is saying in Psalm 90 and 2 Peter 3. Time is relative, and this fact is known for a certainty, because time is a relative quantity throughout our universe. This was proven many years ago by Albert Einstein, and nothing has happened to change this fact since then. So when God led Moses to use the word *day* when describing the initial creation, is there anything in the Bible that proves this word *day* is not used as a metaphor to indicate an unknown period of time? Did God use this metaphor knowing that it would be ridiculous to try to explain to the newly freed Hebrew slaves all the finer details of the original creation? Those who spent four hundred years as slaves of Egypt were not exactly Rhodes scholars. For the most part, they were illiterate and uneducated, and they had been taught the myths and fables about the gods of ancient Egypt. God's purpose in writing the first few chapters of Genesis was to teach the Hebrew slaves that He was the true God and Creator of all, and to indicate that all that they may have learned in Egypt about the gods and creation was only fiction and fable. In conclusion, it is my opinion that the word *day* as used by God to refer to the stages of creation does not mean the literal twenty-four-hour day as we humans may understand.

Now let us discuss the *chronology* of the Old Testament. Was it given for the purpose of accurately dating the time of creation? Bishop Ussher (1581–1656), a famous Irish theologian, merely assumed that the time from Adam to Abraham was calculated simply by the addition of the times between the father and his descendant son in the lists provided in Genesis chapters 5 and 11. He calculated from these genealogical lists that the world was created on October 24, 4004 BC, at 9:30 a.m. His conclusion was later added to the margins of the King James Version of the Bible popular in his day and was accepted by the believing world as biblical fact.

B. B. Warfield wrote, "But for the whole space of time before Abraham, we are dependent entirely on inferences drawn from the genealogies recorded in the fifth and eleventh chapters of Genesis.[15] The chronological suggestion is thus purely the effect of the arrangement of the names in *immediate sequence*; and is not intrinsically resident in the items of information themselves"[16] (emphasis added).

An interesting fact that complicates the idea arises when we read the genealogical lists in Genesis 11. We discover that ten generations are listed before the flood and ten likewise after the flood. If one studies the genealogical lists in the Gospel of Matthew, chapter 1, one discovers three lists of fourteen names each. It seems that the Hebrew authors preferred abridgment when making long lists. Another problem crops up when one examines the priestly lists in 1 Chronicles 6, as compared to Ezra 7. There are a bunch of missing names. In an effort to reduce the number of printed pages in this present volume, I prefer not to provide these two priestly lists and suggest instead that the reader look them over and satisfy his or her own curiosity. Bishop Ussher assumed that the biblical genealogical lists were complete, without error, but as one can see, he made a grievously unsubstantiated assumption.

Another interesting problem arises when looking over the genealogical lists, and that is the descendants of Cain. This problem is the record of Tubal-Cain as recorded in Genesis 4:22. Tubal-Cain was the son of Lamech by his wife Zillah. There are two other descendants who are brothers of Tubal-Cain, and they are Jabal (the father of those who dwell in tents and have livestock) and Jubal (the father of those who play the lyre and pipe). Notice that Tubal-Cain's brothers are recorded as "fathers of" a class of people. Now all that is said about Tubal-Cain is that he was a worker of brass and iron. The text does not mention that he was the father of those who work with brass and iron. There is a problem here. Bishop Ussher helps us out by providing the approximate time of Tubal-Cain, and that date is about 3400 BC. Assuming that Bishop Ussher is correct, here is the problem. Based on the best archeological records, brass was not discovered/ developed until about 3000 BC, approximately. Tubal-Cain lived in the time of the late Stone Age, just like the native Americans when "discovered" by Christopher Columbus. In addition, Tubal-Cain was not a worker of iron, because the discovery of the process used to produce iron was not made until about 1200 BC, approximately.

This account of Tubal-Cain suggests that Genesis 1–11 concerns episodes of Hebrew history and is not necessarily the chronology of Hebrew history. We may conclude that what is recorded about these episodes is correct, but we may not expect the serial construction, that is, the chronological sequence or timing, of the events to be correct. I propose that to the ancient Hebrew mind the fact of an episode may be more important than the sequence of an episode. The Bible records history, but not with the degree of accuracy that we expect in this modern age.

Let's now look at a few unusual words used in the Hebrew Old Testament, with the intent of understanding the meaning of these words and how they may affect our understanding of the text. The first example is in Genesis 6:14, where we find the word *pitch*. "Make for yourself an ark of gopher wood; you shall make the ark with rooms, and shall cover it inside and out with *pitch*."

The original word in the Hebrew Bible is כֹּפֶר (pronounced as "kofer"). Basically, the word means "cover." It can be found as a verb as well as a noun. The word is used in the Old Testament to illustrate God's sanctifying work in covering the sins of the faithful. That is, it is used in reference to the idea of atonement. It is understood why God would use this word when He commanded Noah to cover the ark with this black, gooey, sticky stuff in order to seal the seams of the ark and make it watertight.

The pitch that God was referring to in Genesis 6:14 is a product of biological decomposition, referred to as tar, petroleum, bitumen, or asphalt, a brown or black tar-like substance found in the natural state underground.[17] This pitch is a petrochemical material that was found in many places around the earth, the same stuff found in oil wells, and it is a sludge derived from the decay of a biomass in the ancient earth. It is the remains of biological decomposition and decay from once living plants and tissue. A swamp like the Florida Everglades has a base called a bog. The bog is the accumulation of many years of vegetation that has fallen to the ground and is in the process of decay. In time, this bog turns into a gooey mess that becomes buried under many more tons of decayed vegetation. In time, the gooey bog is compressed into peat, a more solid form of the bog material. After enough time has passed, the peat is compressed into a gooey black mess that we call pitch. Given millions of more years, the pressure becomes so great that it turns the peat/pitch into what the Native Americans called "the stone that burns," and what we call coal, a fossil stone.

Based on the depth and fossil remnants found with it, pitch/peat is considered to be millions of years old. Pitch is commonly found in the Middle East; large deposits have been found under the Dead Sea. This is why the Arabian Desert is so rich in oil, which is sold worldwide to power our modern transportation systems. Our asphalt roads are made from this pitch. Millions of years ago the Arabian Desert was a flowering paradise with plenty of water and foliage, but because of climate changes, we now can use distilled pitch to power our automobiles. We call it gasoline. We can conclude that pitch is a fossil remnant from millions of years ago, and we can give thanks to God for having created all those wonderful dinosaurs that now feed our modern economy.

The following subject is another translation issue that reveals that God accommodated His readers' understanding of their world and chose not to teach about the universe in a way that was beyond their scientific understanding. So we begin with the question, is there a hard dome-like shell holding back waters above the earth as the Bible seems to indicate? The King James Version of the Bible and the New King James translation both use the word *firmament* as a translation in Genesis 1:6 for the word רקיע (pronounced as "ra-kee-a," *Strongest* #7549). The word occurs seventeen times in the Old Testament and is translated as "firmament" every time in the King James Version of the Bible. The old American Standard Version Bible (1901) also uses the word *firmament* in this verse. The New American Standard Version translates the verse as thus: "Let there be an *expanse* in the midst of the waters" (emphasis added). The English Standard Version, and the New International Version also translate this word as "expanse." The Revised Standard Version and the New Revised Standard Version of the Bible translate this word as "dome." The Living Bible uses the word *space* as the acceptable translation, and the popular Bible translation called The Message translates this word as "sky." So which is it?

William D. Mounce defines this word as "expanse; the space above the earth that holds visible objects: clouds, planets, stars."[18] A further definition refers to "the vault of heaven," or "firmament" as regarded by the Hebrews, as a solid dome supporting waters above the sky,[19] a solid surface, beaten metallic surface that supports the waters above it. The *Jewish Study Bible* defines this word as "expanse," referring to a piece of metal that has been hammered into a thin shiny dome and that is used to separate the waters in the sky from the waters below.[20]

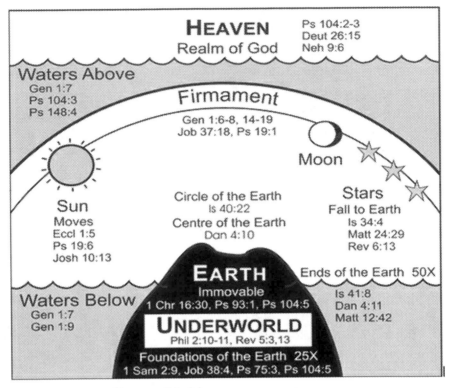

FIGURE 8.1 MAP OF THE FIRMAMENT

The LXX (the Old Testament Greek translation from about 200 BC) uses the Greek word *sterewma*, which means "solid, firm, metallic, etc." The conclusion simply is that the author is referencing the primitive idea that the earth is flat and that there is a dome over the earth that holds up the heavens and also the water that falls as rain. The *Theological Dictionary of the Old Testament* adds further definition when it states, "'ra-kee-a' denotes a stable, solid entity situated above the earth, which protects the living world from an influx of the waters of chaos. The noun bears the connotation 'compact, firm' so that translations such as 'expanse' miss the mark."[21]

"The basic historical fact that defines the meaning of *ra-kee-a* in Genesis One is simply this: all peoples in the ancient world thought of the sky as solid."[22] In Genesis 7:11 we read, "And the floodgates of the sky were opened." In ancient thought, it was necessary to open up the vault of heaven, the firmament, to allow the waters from heaven (the sky) to fall as rain and also to flood the earth. The ancients believed that rain came from the heaven above the firmament. They just did not understand the evaporation cycle of the earth's weather system.

Some verses that teach the idea of a dome above the earth are as follows:

> "Can you, with Him, spread out the skies, Strong as a *molten mirror*?" (Job 37:18, emphasis added).

Note the phrase "molten mirror." In ancient times, they could not make glass with which to fashion a modern mirror. Instead, they would polish a piece of brass, thereby making it very shiny and reflective. Then they could see their face in the mirror. Also, when they melted the brass over a hot fire, the molten brass was very reflective, thereby serving as an excellent mirror.

> "The One who builds His upper chambers in the heavens and has founded His vaulted dome over the earth" (Amos 9:6).

> "Now over the heads of the living beings there was something like an expanse, like the awesome gleam of crystal, spread out over their heads" (Ezekiel 1:22).

Much of the ancient world believed that the earth was flat and that the sky was held up by something solid. Records show that the ancient Sumerians, Babylonians, Egyptian, Hittites, Indians, Chinese, Africans, and Native Americans held to a view that the gods placed a solid dome between the heavens and the sky above the earth. Even the ancient Greek philosophers held to such an idea.

> "When the original readers of Genesis 1 read the word *ra-kee-a*, they thought of a solid sky. ... Historical evidence shows that virtually everyone in the ancient world believed in a solid firmament."[23]

Samuel Noah Kramer, noted scholar of ancient history, wrote in his book *History Begins at Sumer* (which is a study of the most ancient known civilization, Sumer, from about 3500 BC) the following conclusion: "The earth, they thought, was a flat disk, heaven, a hollow space enclosed at top and bottom by a solid surface in the shape of a vault."[24] I highly recommend that any further interest in this subject should lead one to consult the *Westminster Theological Journal* that is referenced in note number 22, listed at the end of this chapter.

I find it interesting that the great Jewish writer and philosopher Josephus (first century AD) wrote in his book *The Antiquities of the Jews* the following: "After this, on the second day, he placed the heaven over the whole world, and separated it from the other parts, and he determined it should stand by itself. He also placed a crystalline [firmament] round it, and put it together in a manner agreeable to the earth, and fitted it for giving moisture and rain, and for affording the advantage of dews."[25]

So we see that Josephus believed that Genesis 1:6 was referring to a solid barrier that separated the heavens and the waters above the earth. Again we see that God directed the writing of scripture to reveal spiritual truth, and in doing thus, God saw fit to accommodate the ignorance of the age and not dwell on the actual physical facts of His creation, which would be confusing to readers in the fourteenth century BC.

The question we need to ask today is, how can we send a rocket to the moon if the earth is surrounded by this solid dome? The rocket would crash into this solid dome and fall back to earth. The KJV translates this word as "firmamentum," from the Latin equivalent in the Vulgate Bible. A Latin classical dictionary defines this word as "a means of support, a prop." In my opinion, this is a better translation because it accurately explains the meaning of the original Hebrew word (רקיע). This translation problem can explain why it is not always proper to literally interpret the words of an English translation of the Bible as the YECs always do, but instead, as a matter of accuracy, to always base our understanding on the original manuscripts and language as much as possible. Further, our understanding of the text must always be based on proper hermeneutical principles.

Another translation problem is found in Genesis 2:8: "The Lord God planted a garden toward the *east*, in Eden; and there He placed the man whom He had formed" (emphasis added).

The word *east* is the Hebrew word *qadem* (קֶדֶם) (מִקֶּדֶם*Strong's* #6924a).[26] The word is found sixty-two times in the Old Testament. About thirty-two times the word is translated as "aforetime," "past time," "former time," "antiquity," "ancient time," "from of old," or "in front of"; and thirty times it is translated as "east." So how should we interpret this passage? It turns out that the word *qedem* has a dual meaning. It can be interpreted as "east" or as "ancient, before time, antiquity." Now the problem lies with the presuppositions that the translators had. Is the word *qadem* a temporal word referencing time, or is it a word referencing direction? The phrase "God planted a garden towards the east" just doesn't make sense. The question is, east of what? The obvious question one asks is, what does the concept of east mean in this verse; east of what? East is a direction, not a destination, so the verse literally says, in the English text, that God planted a garden in the east, a direction. If one travels east long enough, he will return to where he started, knowing that one can circle the globe by just traveling long enough in one direction. So, it does not make sense to our Western minds that we could understand that something is placed at or in the east.

However, the phrase "God planted a garden from antiquity" does make sense. Also, one must notice that the word in the text of Genesis 2:8 contains the preposition *min* (מִן), which is a Hebrew preposition translated as "from" and which designates an ablative case or "source." This frequent preposition is best translated as "from."[27] The *Theological Word Book of the Old Testament* states, "The noun *qedem* has either a geographical meaning 'east' or a temporal (time related) notion, meaning ancient time, aforetime, ancient past, in front of, etc."[28] Further confirmation of this interpretation is found in the *Theological Dictionary of the Old Testament* where we read, "Parallel to its spatial meaning, *qedem* also refers to a time prior to that of the observer, either relatively in the sense of 'earlier' or absolutely in the sense of prehistoric times, primeval time."[29]

I believe one can conclude that another possible and preferred translation for Genesis 2:8 would be,

> "The Lord God planted a garden from ancient times
> in Eden; and there He placed the man whom He had
> formed." Therefore the translation "from ancient times"
> is a proven and acceptable rendition of Genesis 2:8.[30]

Several other examples where the word *qedem* is used to imply old age or ancient times occur in Isaiah 45:21, Isaiah 46:10, and Proverbs 8:22. This leaves us with the conclusion that Eden, the garden of God, was created long before humankind (possibly before Genesis 1), and was placed somewhere on earth, perhaps in the Mesopotamian valley. If this is correct, then the YECs have a new problem to explain. If Eden was placed on earth in the ancient times, then the earth had to have been created long before humankind.

However, thus far we have not eliminated the confusion when we agree that the word in question can represent both time and direction. We have clearly shown that the proposed translation, "from ancient times," is the preferred rendering of the phrase from Hebrew to English. Then a question still lingers concerning why in some passages the word *qedem* is translated as "east." An explanation is related to the ancient Hebrew concept of time. The ancient Hebrews (as well as other ancient peoples) thought of the past as being before them, or in front of their faces. In fact, the root meaning of the word *qedem* is given as "in front, before, foreword, etc."[31] The ancients saw the future as behind them, because it could not be seen, and the past in front of them, because the past could be seen. From this concept, the word came to mean "that which was past." Further, in the ancient mind, the past was represented by looking east, since that was where the day began with the rising of the sun. From this analogy, the word *qedem* acquired the additional meaning of direction, toward the east, which was the past, or the beginning of the day.

Another word for study is the word *Eden* [עֵדֶן] (*Strongest NASB* #5731), the name found in scripture that indicates the paradise that God created for humankind. It is found fourteen times in the Old Testament, is identified as a place of "pleasure, delight," and is pictured as a fertile area, a well-watered oasis with large trees, which is a very attractive prospect in the arid east.[32] Ancients, historians, and archeologists have searched in vain for centuries, looking to find some evidence of the existence of Eden, all to no avail. I am of the opinion that humankind will never find Eden because it is no longer on earth. Being the garden of God, His abode, Eden, we are not wrong to assume, is actually heaven or a part of heaven and is eternal with God.

Remember where we read in Revelation 21 about the city of God coming down to earth? Could it be that Eden is part of that city where God sits upon His throne? I am of the opinion that the faithful, the elect of God, will someday rest in the garden from whence fallen humankind was ejected. Remember that the cherubim (Genesis 3:24) were placed at the entrance of the garden of God, of Eden, to prevent humankind from entering again, eating of the tree of life, and living forever against God's direct judgment. Obviously, if Eden could still be found on earth, it would be necessary for the cherubim to be continuously protecting it. That would attract a large crowd of spectators. Someday Jesus will come and all these things will be known!

When God said that *"it was good"* for each day of creation, what did He mean? Was it morally good or functionally good? The YECs claim that the Bible uses the word *good* in Genesis 1 to show that there was no sin upon the earth during the creation week. It is interesting to consider that the YECs ignore a more probable interpretation, which is that God used the word *good* to explain that each act of creation was successful in fulfilling God's purpose. The YECs want to convince everyone that Paul's statement in Romans 5:12—"Therefore, just as through one man sin entered into the world, and death through sin, and so death spread to all men, because all sinned"—implies that death came upon all of God's creation following Adam's (the man's) sin, and that was not good. The YECs suggest that all life was created to live forever and therefore there was no need for the tree of life situated in the midst of the garden. The truth is that humankind were to live forever by eating from the tree of life. Read Genesis 3:24. The YECs suggest that dinosaurs died because of humankind's sin, yet the text clearly states that it was "men" who died as the result of Adam's sin. Answers in Genesis states repeatedly that dinosaurs lived with Adam and Eve before the Fall. All one has to do is look at the fossil remains of most dinosaurs and examine the giant teeth that they had, because these teeth were designed to rip and tear flesh. Then one will discover that the statements Answers in Genesis provides are wrong. If the dinosaurs were alive in Adam's day, we would not be here today. The dinosaurs, like the T. rex, were voracious carnivorous eaters for which human beings would be a delicious treat.

One time God used the phrase "not good," and that was in reference to the situation when the man was alone. The text strongly implies that

God had designed man for a mate, a woman, and it was not good that the man should be alone. Next, look at Genesis 1:24, which reads, "Let the *earth* bring forth living creatures." Is this referring to biological evolution? Now we know without a doubt that it was God who created all things, yet why did He choose to state in Genesis 1:24 that the earth brought forth living animals? Biologically this is true, as we know that all flesh is made up of the elements and minerals found on planet Earth, yet God choose to imply that the earth was the cause of creation. This causes one to wonder what God is trying to teach us.

Let's look at another concept. Rather than insisting on the immediate creation of life in an instant or in a twelve-hour period, would we be amiss to suggest that the duration of the creation process is a mystery not revealed to us at this time? We must acknowledge that God did it, in His time and in His way, but does the book of Genesis provide all the detail we would like about the timing and process of creation? No? Then why should we argue about God's timing and process of creation? I believe it is clear we were not provided enough information to arrive at a full explanation.

In light of the subjects we covered in this chapter, let's now look at how some will distort true science just in an attempt a prove a recent creation by using a misguided view of Scripture and science.

[1]   Stephen Hawking, *A Brief History of Time* (New York: Bantam Books, 2001), 44.

[2]   *Barashith* in the first clause is a *prepositional phrase*, the theme of the first clause, and this clause is the theme of the text. W. Dennis Tucker, ed., *Genesis 1–11*, vol. 1 of *Baylor Handbook on the Hebrew Bible* (Waco, TX: Baylor University Press, 2008), 42.

[3]   *JPS Hebrew–English Tanakh* (Philadelphia: Jewish Publication Society, 1999).

[4]   Richard E. Friedman, *Commentary on the Torah* (New York: HarperOne, 2003), 3.

[5]   John Sailhamer, *Genesis Unbound* (Colorado Springs: Dawson Media, 2011), 42.

[6]   Merrill C. Tenney, ed., *The Zondervan Pictorial Encyclopedia of the Bible*, vol. 1 (Grand Rapids, MI: Zondervan, 1975), 1022.

[7]   E. Wurthwein, *The Text of the Old Testament* (Grand Rapids, MI: Eerdmans, 1979), 21.

[8]   William G. T. Shedd, *Dogmatic Theology* (Minneapolis: Klock & Klock Publishers, 1979; reprint of original by Charles Scribner's Sons, 1889), 475.

[9]   Gregg R. Allison, *Historical Theology: An Introduction to Christian Doctrine* (Grand Rapids, MI: Zondervan, 2011), 259.

[10] Shedd, *Dogmatic Theology*, 476.

[11] Herman Bavinck, *Our Reasonable Faith* (Grand Rapids, MI: Baker Books, 1978), 172.

[12] Gleason L. Archer, *A Survey of Old Testament Introduction* (Chicago: Moody Press, 1974), 186.

[13] M. J. Erickson, *Christian Theology* (Grand Rapids, MI: Baker Book House, 1985), 382.

[14] L. Berkhof, *Systematic Theology* (Grand Rapids, MI: Eerdmans, 1974), 153.

[15] B. B. Warfield, *Biblical and Theological Studies* (Philadelphia: Presbyterian and Reformed, 1968), 240.

[16] Warfield, 244.

[17] R. Laird Harris, ed., *Theological Wordbook of the Old Testament*, vol. 1 (Chicago: Moody Press, 1980), 453.

[18] William D. Mounce, *Mounce's Complete Expository Dictionary of Old & New Testament Words* (Grand Rapids, MI: Zondervan, 2006), 1045.

[19] Francis Brown, S.R.Driver, and C.A.Briggs, *Hebrew and English Lexicon of the Old Testament* (Oxford: Clarendon Press, 1978), 956.

[20] *The Jewish Study Bible* (New York: Jewish Publication Society, Oxford Press, 1999), 13.

[21] G. J. Botterweck et al., *Theological Dictionary of the Old Testament*, vol. 13 (Grand Rapids, MI: Eerdmans, 2004), 649.

[22] *Westminster Theological Journal* 53 (1991): 228.

[23] *Westminster Theological Journal*, 236.

[24] Samuel N. Kramer, *History Begins at Sumer* (London: Thames & Hudson, 1961), 120.

[25] William Whiston, ed., "Chapter 1," in *Works of Flavius Josephus, Book I*, vol. 2 (Grand Rapids, MI: Baker Book House, 1978), 1.

[26] Robert L. Thomas, ed., *The Strongest NASB Exhaustive Concordance* (Grand Rapids, MI: Zondervan, 1998), 1463.

[27] G. D. Pratico and M. V. Van Pelt, *Basics of Biblical Hebrew Grammar* (Grand Rapids, MI: Zondervan, 2007), 52.

[28] R. Laird Harris, ed., *Theological Wordbook of the Old Testament*, vol. 2 (Chicago: Moody Press, 1980), 785.

[29] G. Johannes Botterweck, ed., *Theological Dictionary of the Old Testament*, vol. 12 (Grand Rapids, MI: Eerdmans, 2012), 508.

[30] G. J. Wenham, *Genesis 1–15*, vol. 1 of *Word Biblical Commentary* (Waco, TX: Word Books, 1987) (ref. to qedem), 61.

[31] Brown, Driver, and Briggs, *Hebrew and English Lexicon*, 869.

[32] G. J. Wenham, *Word Biblical Commentary* (Waco, TX: Word Books, 1987) (ref. to *beginning, first, rasheth*), 13.

CHAPTER 9

Examples of Fraudulent Science

It is not my purpose in this chapter to question the inspiration of the Bible or its accuracy and authority. It is, however, my purpose to show how the Bible has been used to support false conclusions about the creation of the world and universe. Well-intentioned people have used the Bible to support their personal concepts of God's creation, and in so doing they have left the realm of reality for a new realm of fiction. The principal example of a nonscientific method is when someone will observe a phenomenon and then try to find an idea to explain it in order to fit a preconceived idea. In this case, the preconceived idea is a six-thousand-year-old universe.

One of the persistent issues faced by those schooled in science and the scientific method is that of the young earth creationist's (YEC) approach to the problem of coordinating the world's physical data to fit their preconceived notion of a young earth. It seems that the YECs will make any attempt to fit physical data into a young earth paradigm. When one shows them how wrong they are in their conclusions, they will then attempt another explanation with invented excuses. They refuse to stop coming up with irrational reasons to support their argument. So far, they have continually failed, but they go back to the Bible searching for what they call "scientific evidence" to support their positions. If they fail in this effort, then they insist that the phenomena are miracles, thereby eliminating any counterpoint argument. The YECs base their arguments on a simple conclusion: that the date of the creation in Genesis 1 can be calculated by adding up the years during which the biblical ancestors listed in Genesis chapters 5, 10, and 11 lived.

However, please read what some very notable Bible scholars have to say about the idea of dating events recorded in the Bible by adding up the years of the ancient fathers listed in the book of Genesis. In the book *Genesis Unbound* by Dr. John Sailhamer, we read, "The dating of creation based on the genealogies of Genesis 5 and 10 is faulty for the following two reasons, One; It assumes that the biblical genealogies are to be understood as strict chronologies, and Two; It assumes that the beginning of creation occurred on the first day of the week."[1]

In his book *The Pentateuch in Its Cultural Environment*, Dr. G. Herbert Livingston makes two very important comments, as follows: "To hold that Genesis 1–11 is more than historic, that it contains accounts of events that really happened, traditional scholars have been faced with several problems. The first is that there were no human eye witnesses present to behold and record the creation events in Genesis 1 up to man's own creation by God ... and the second problem that faces traditional scholars is the fact that Genesis 1–11 is not an encyclopedia of data about people, places and chronology."[2]

An important point to understand is that the Bible is a theological treatise, not a history book (even though it contains historical events). Its principal purpose is to reveal Almighty God to humankind, not to teach humankind the history of the universe or the science of the universe.

At this point I want to explain to the reader that I will make frequent references to known scientific facts and conclusions. I realize that some of the readers of *And There Was Light* will not be familiar with all of these scientific axioms and perhaps have not been trained in science, so I will at appropriate moments have to spend time explaining the science behind the data that helps us to develop our conclusions and come to a firm knowledge of the age of God's creation.

Let me state first that science, as I will explain, is more like a verb and less like a noun. Simply put, *science is the observation of the natural phenomena of God's created universe and the formulation of laws or formulas that explain or predict the observed natural phenomena.* As a verb, science is *what one does* in formulating the laws or formulas of observed natural phenomena. Remember, a verb denotes an action, not a belief. Science is not a belief system unless one decides to accept by faith opinions concerning observed natural phenomena, minus the physical proof. False science is where one accepts unproven opinions concerning observed natural phenomena. An example of false science is the belief that the earth is flat and that it does not move in the universe. I know this may be hard to accept, but those believing in a flat earth are more numerous than many would suspect. At this point, one may read again chapter 2 of *And There Was Light* in order to clarify the proper method of scientific research. On occasion I have to cringe when someone will refer to a logical process as being scientific. I remember hearing in seminary a professor state that systematic theology is a science. Systematic theology may be based on logical, rational thinking, but it is *not* a science, because it is based on unprovable conclusions, for example, that the Bible is the "Word of God." I truly believe that claim, but my belief is based on a presuppositional faith, not on the scientific method, as there is no way to prove the object of my faith.

I need to add one more point. In the famous televised debate a few years ago between Ken Ham of Answers in Genesis (a ministry) and Bill Nye, a well-known science teacher, Mr. Ham mentioned that there are two types of science: (1) observational science and (2) historical science. Now to the educated and trained scientist, this statement by Mr. Ham surely came as a complete surprise, as this idea doesn't occur anywhere in the libraries of science. Mr. Ham's argument goes like this: since the age of the universe preceded the age of humankind, no one was around to confirm the English Bible story of creation, and therefore we must assume that the highly abbreviated creation story as found in the popular English Bibles must be true since it can't be confirmed through scientific inquiry. In other words, any study of the concept of creation is meddling with historical science and any conclusions drawn cannot be substantiated. Observational science, according to Mr. Ham, is science conducted in the laboratories under human observation and whose results can be confirmed. So Mr. Ham simply dismisses all scientific results or conclusions concerning the beginning of the heavens and the earth since there was no one to observe it.

I wonder if Mr. Ham has ever heard of forensic science. I ask because forensic science is the application of scientific knowledge and methodology to legal problems of a historical nature, that is, *after* the crime has been committed, sometimes many, many years afterward. In fact forensic science techniques have been used to solve ancient mysteries from hundreds, if not thousands, of years ago, one example being the examining of evidence in ancient Egyptian tombs to discover how the corpse met its end. So this is just one of many examples where scientific principles can be used to recover facts pertaining to events that happened in the ancient past. The laws of physics do not change over time. They have always been the same from creation. An explanation of forensic science shows that it encompasses many different fields of science, including physics, anthropology, biology, chemistry, engineering, geology, genetics, and medicine. Therefore, Mr. Ham is wrong in his opinions about science.

Now let's begin by giving some examples of popular false science as understood by some Christians or as propagated by the claims of the YECs and Answers in Genesis (AIG).

"Radiometric dating is wrong because isotope decay is not constant."

This claim is one of the most obnoxious claims that the YECs make. Their purpose is to spread distrust among the general public, especially Christians, and, thereby discredit any findings from reputable sources. Yes, when radiometric dating was first discovered many years ago, there were mistakes made by untrained technicians. However, as the years passed and new and better laboratory equipment was added, alongside better training for the lab assistants, the results for radiometric dating became much more consistent. Any test of the age of a material in question is repeated many times using different methods in order to arrive at a consensus for the age of the material. Only then are the results published. Therefore, in this modern scientific age, radiometric dating results can be trusted. I cover the topic of radiometric dating in detail in chapter 6 of *And There Was Light*. The reader may review that chapter again at this point.

Now I want to offer a rebuttal of a comment I found in a book by Jonathan Sarfati entitled *Refuting Compromise*. In chapter 11 of his book, Sarfati tries to show that the decay rate of the atomic nucleus varies over time; therefore, it is not possible to use inconsistent half-lives of radioactive isotopes to date the creation of the earth or universe. Sarfati seems to suggest that heat, pressure, gravity, or whatever has affected the rate of decay for many or most radioactive isotopes, thereby making the results of no use in dating the creation. Then he goes on to suggest an absurd idea: "The best answer seems to be an episode of accelerated nuclear decay, during creation week or the flood year, or more likely both."[3]

This idea is impossible. Having a degree in chemistry, Jonathan Sarfati should know better. Temperature or pressure cannot affect any rate of change in the decay of the nucleus of an atom. The nucleus of an atom is held together by the strongest force known to humankind. The rate of decay for an atomic nucleus is a function of *quantum* physics and it can't be changed. The reason is simply that the decay rate is a function of the strong nuclear force holding the atomic nucleus together. When one splits the atomic nucleus, an enormous amount of energy is released, as witnessed in the detonation of an atomic bomb. When you get down to the size of the atomic nucleus, large-scale physics no longer works. Max Planck, a world-renowned physicist from the early twentieth century, discovered quantum physics, the field of study of the very small world, the world of the atomic nucleus. The nucleus of an atom is not influenced by heat or pressure. Mr. Sarfati's response is a perfect example of fraudulent science. The reader must be aware by now that the YECs will come up with any idea to support their conviction that the world was created in 144 hours, just six thousand years ago. If they can't support their claim with facts, then they will fall back on the claim that God did it through a miracle. I agree that creation was a miracle, but it did not happen six thousand years ago. If Mr. Sarfati would like to join me, we can visit one of the major universities near my home and then resolve his confusion by seeking advice from some of our well-known scientists on the subject.

"Dinosaurs lived with Adam and Eve."

The following is a quotation from the Answers in Genesis web page: "Imagine dinosaurs living with people. The thought sounds ludicrous to a modern mind steeped in evolution. But it's the only reasonable conclusion if the Bible is true." If Adam and Eve had to live with the dinosaurs of long ago, as Ken Ham and AIG insist, then my question is, how did they survive? AIG claims that dinosaurs ate only vegetables before the flood. Of course they can't prove that; they just make the guess in order to "support" their interpretation of Genesis 1 in the English Bible. I have visited many museums of paleontology and the dinosaur skeletons that I saw would be picking their teeth with the bones of Adam and Eve if dinosaurs and human beings had lived together. What is even more absurd is the idea that the dinosaurs had to live with Noah and his family aboard the ark for the better part of a year.

Please refer to figure 5.2 in chapter 5, the picture of the T. rex that I took at the Hot Springs County Pioneer Museum in Thermopolis, Wyoming,[4] a few years back. Now I want to ask the reader, can anyone imagine how long a person could survive living with a monster such as this? *Notice the teeth.* They are not used for eating grass as the staff of AIG would tell you. No, these teeth were designed to rip and tear flesh, as this T. rex did during its lifetime. That's a terrible way to die. *Tyrannosaurus rex* is just one of thousands of types of "terrible lizards" that lived during the Jurassic period of the earth (about 150 million to 200 million years before Christ). Answers in Genesis says that Noah had a pair of every kind of animal aboard the ark. The question is, how did he keep them from eating each other? Again, the YECs will appeal to a miracle by God, where all the animals aboard the ark were put into a hibernation state by God, or God selected only the baby animals, thereby reducing the task of feeding, or … or … The list of miracles gets very long when the YECs are trying to win the argument for a young earth.

"Dinosaur bones are not found with human bones."

Now if dinosaurs coexisted with humans, or hominoids (humanlike beasts), or apes, or any large mammals, then there would be a fossil record of both dinosaurs and humankind, or humanlike animals or other large mammals buried together. No such record exists. There are thirty-five archeological digs just in the mountain regions of Thermopolis, Wyoming alone. In these digs are found many ancient forms of creatures that we often refer to as dinosaurs. I know because I visited there a few years ago and I have seen these digs. There has been no discovery of mammal bones or human bones in any of these digs. The mountain regions of the West are full of hundreds of dinosaur digs, and no human remains have been found with any of the dinosaur fossils. This fact leads one to believe that humans did not live during the age of the giant reptiles.

There exists a simple reason for this archeological fact. All ancient dinosaur and giant reptile fossils have been found below the K-T boundary, and mammal fossils and human remains have been found above this boundary. Now we need a word of explanation. When you dig into the ground and find relics or bones from a prior age, you can safely conclude that the relics found in the deepest part of the dig were deposited at an earlier time than were the relics found near the surface of the dig. That is just common sense. The land on which we live is not fixed; it is always being moved and modified, and material is being added to or removed from it through wind and rain erosion. Most people would not see this change on the earth around where they live because it takes a lot of time for these things to happen, often more than several lifetimes. So the fact is this: as the soil is added or shifted from various landscapes, the soil is deposited in layers. As time goes by more layers are added, and this results in a stratification of the soil. When you are traveling down the highways of the United States, especially those out west, you will see road-cuts where the original earth and stone is visible. There you will see (in most cases) the clear strata lines. Those lines nearest the top represent the recent layers, and those strata lines near the bottom represent the oldest layers. This is one of the ways that geologists and archeologists date the fossils, by dating the layer (or stratum) in which the fossil was found. Some of the most profound strata lines are clearly seen in the Grand Canyon.

Using the best dating techniques possible, paleontologists have determined that the dinosaurs went extinct about sixty-five million years ago. Humankind was not created at that time. The first piece of evidence was the discovery of a layer of a rare element known as iridium (atomic weight 77). This element is a very rare metal, seldom found on earth. It is most often found in meteorites. This layer of iridium is found in a thin layer all over the earth, and it marks the K-T boundary. Everywhere one digs, one will find this layer of gray material containing iridium. Reason tells us that in order for there to be common results, there must have been a common cause. Therefore scientists searched for the common cause, knowing that the answer had to be a giant meteorite that hit the planet, because that is the only reason for such a large deposit of iridium. After years of searching for a very large meteor, geologists discovered a massive crater located off the Yucatán Peninsula in the Gulf of Mexico, near the village of Chicxulub. The size of meteorite that caused the crater would have to have been between six and ten miles wide, and it would have had to travel at such a tremendous speed to cause giant earthquakes, tsunamis, acid rain, global darkness, and a worldwide winter. Geologists have calculated the original crater left by the impact as being about 110 miles wide and 20 miles deep into the earth. The evidence is buried in the rock formations. This meteoric event led to the death of most life on planet Earth, including the dinosaurs and other giant reptiles. This is the reason that dinosaur bones are always found below the K-T boundary, and why the bones of human beings, who arrived on earth much later, are always found above the K-T boundary. The phrase *K-T* refers to the Cretaceous (K – 150 million to 65 million years ago) and the Tertiary (T – 62,000 to 1 million years ago) periods. The YECs are wrong again.

"An airplane sank in the ice of Greenland."

In his book *Refuting Compromise*, Jonathan Sarfati brings up the subject of some World War II airplanes[5] that crash-landed on the ice sheet of Greenland. I have read about this before and about the aviation enthusiasts who dug into the ice to free the plane so that it could be taken back to the United States to be restored and placed in an aviation museum. The plane in question was a Boeing B-29 Superfortress. It crashed in 1947 on the Greenland ice cap while on a secret Cold War mission. The YECs' argument is that the thickness of the Greenland ice sheet (over seven thousand feet, and up to ten thousand feet thick maximum) is no indication of the age of the earth because the B-29 had sunk more than two hundred feet down into the ice sheet since 1947. A team was set out to retrieve the plane in 2014, sixty-seven years after it had been lost. The YECs believe that since the airplane sank into the ice two hundred feet in sixty-seven years, this fact proves that the earth is young, like perhaps only six thousand years, and it doesn't take thousands of years for layers of ice to accumulate.

Well, the YECs need to do some work on their understanding of basic science. This episode reminds me of the time I needed to mark the location of my buried radio transmitting cable in my backyard. I sat an eight-inch red brick on my lawn to mark the location of the buried cable. As time passed, I noticed that the brick was sinking into the ground. By the time winter arrived, the brick was almost completely buried. Today, I can't find the brick because it has sunk completely out of sight. The truth is that gravity rules!

Now about the airplane. The B-29 weighed a little more than fifty tons empty. The plane started sinking into the ice the moment it landed. If anyone wants to check this out, just squeeze an ice cube in a vice and watch it melt. Water freezes at 32°F, but under pressure, it will melt even at a lower temperature. The fifty-ton airplane spent sixty-seven years sinking into the ice cap of Greenland just like the red brick sunk into my grass-filled backyard. The depth to which the airplane sank into the ice has nothing to do with the age of the Greenland ice cap. The Greenland ice cap has been measured to be about 10,800 feet thick at its deepest point and has been dated to a little older than 110,000 years old. The dating procedure is based on the number of layers of ice as found in the ice core samples. The annual snowfall in Greenland is very low, just as in Antarctica, because very little snow falls in the extreme cold temperatures. Therefore, to date the ice cap, one needs to count the layers in the ice core samples just as you count tree rings to date the age of trees. The YECs need to rethink their arguments.

"The ages of comets prove a young universe."

The YECs like to bring up their implied proof that the universe is young because comets disintegrate too quickly. The following is a quotation from the Answers in Genesis web page:

> According to evolutionary theory, comets are supposed to be the same age as the solar system, about five billion years [this statement is not true]. Yet each time a comet orbits close to the sun, it loses so much of its material that it could not survive much longer than about

100,000 years [complete speculation]. Many comets have typical ages of less than 10,000 years [again, complete speculation]. Evolutionists explain this discrepancy by assuming that (a) comets come from an unobserved spherical "Oort cloud" well beyond the orbit of Pluto, (b) improbable gravitational interactions with infrequently passing stars often knock comets into the solar system, and (c) other improbable interactions with planets slow down the incoming comets often enough to account for the hundreds of comets observed. So far, none of these assumptions has been substantiated either by observations or realistic calculations—according to evolutionary theory, the Kuiper Belt would quickly become exhausted if there were no Oort cloud to supply it [where did they come up with this idea?].[6] Enclosed in brackets are my comments.

Much of the argument proposed by Answers in Genesis is founded on assumption or speculation, for which they offer no evidence. Comet-forming material can easily be attributed to the debris floating in our galaxy (the Milky Way) and to the fact that, in time, this material coalesces into solid bodies, mostly made up of methane ice, water ice, dust, rocks, and other space debris. It is true that comets lose material every time they pass by the sun, but the YECs have no idea how many possible comets are actually out in the Kuiper Belt. The Kuiper Belt has been assumed for years to be the primary source of comets, and there may still be enough comet material out there to last millions more years. No one knows. The Kuiper Belt is a belt of material the lies in a plane surrounding our solar system. The ex-planet Pluto is suspected of being a Kuiper Belt member. Therefore the YECs' argument reveals their ignorance. Show me the evidence that the number of comets could not last much more than ten thousand to one hundred thousand years. AIG has no such evidence. Most comet material that we know of lies in the Kuiper Belt and may never enter into the inner solar system. Also, many comets enter the solar system, only to crash into the sun. NASA has posted photographic material on the internet to show this evidence.

Next, the YECs like to bring up the subject of the Oort cloud that is a suggested source for comets. The proposed Oort cloud (named after the astronomer who suggested its existence) is a vast cloud of astronomical debris that surrounds (and also lies far outside of) our solar system in all directions. Its existence has not yet been proven by any observational attempts because it is so very far away. Now I would like to make a suggestion to the YECs that it is not necessary to see the Oort cloud in order to prove its existence. When a comet or any other astronomical body enters our solar system close enough to be seen with our telescopes, all that is required to prove its source is a measurement of at least three (and possibly more) points of its orbit and then to graphically plot these points (using a computer, of course). These points of the comet's orbit will enable astronomers to calculate the actual orbit and its extent. Then the comet's path through space and its source in question can be determined. All planetary orbits are ellipses, and it only requires a minimum of three points to fix the size and shape of an ellipse; therefore, the actual origin of the body can be determined from the graphical plot, which means that it is not necessary to see the Oort cloud to prove it exists. If the plotted orbit shows that the comet came from a great distance outside the solar system in an orbit perpendicular to the plane of the solar system, then we know the source more than likely is the area of the invisible Oort cloud.

"Many strata are too tightly bent."

The following is a quotation from the Answers in Genesis web page: "In many mountainous areas, strata thousands of feet thick are bent and folded into hairpin shapes. The conventional geologic time scale says these formations were deeply buried and solidified for hundreds of millions of years before they were bent. Yet the folding occurred without cracking, with radii so small that the entire formation had to be still wet and unsolidified when the bending occurred. This implies that the folding occurred *less than thousands of years* after deposition."[7]

The author of this article from the AIG web page could not be more wrong. This article clearly shows that the AIG team desperately lacks scientific talent. On one of my travels to Wyoming several years ago, I ran across a rock feature as described above. I was traveling on I-80 east of

Cheyenne. The rocks that I saw were about a mile north of the freeway. I stopped at a rest stop on the freeway to look at the rock formation because it was so unusual to see. There were several large rocks, about three hundred to five hundred feet high, jutting out of the ground at about a 45-degree angle. These rocks looked like an upside down U. The many layers of strata were clearly visible in these upside-down-U formations. The strata lines clearly showed a sharp 180-degree bend in the rock, with no visible cracks or fracture marks. Well, how did these rocks develop like this? It's simple. At the correct temperature (usually around 1,000 to 1,400 degrees), rocks become like candy taffy or a stick of gum. They become like soft plastic and bend and stretch without cracking or breaking. The geological underground forces heated the rock and pushed the slab of rock up above grade and left the rock bent as a result of the uplifting push from below. The temperature at which rock melts, or softens, also depends on the pressure to which the rock is subjected. As the temperature and/or pressure gets higher, rocks melt just as they are melted in the earth's magma, then the rocks will flow like cold molasses syrup.

How did these unusual rocks end up sticking out of the ground like a giant finger? The eastern half of Wyoming near Cheyenne is about six thousand feet above sea level. Most of the western states of our country rest on the North American geological plate, which is being uplifted. This is the result of the Pacific geological plate plowing under the West Coast and lifting the North American plate up. This action is what causes the earthquakes we see so often out west. Most of the mountain states in the United States rest on this geological plate that is being lifted. That is how the Rocky Mountains were formed.

I should mention at this point that the earth is covered by a crust composed of rock (mostly granite rock). The rocky crust of the earth varies in thickness from approximately five to fifty miles thick, and the crust floats on the magma sea just under it. The magma is more dense and heavier than the crust; therefore, the crust floats on top. Now the crust makes up the continents, and it is a fact proven by geologists for decades that the continents are the geological plates that float on the magma. At this time we know that the Atlantic Ocean is splitting apart at a rate of about one inch per year. The evidence can be seen in the rift in the earth through Iceland and the Mid-Atlantic Ridge (a crack in the seafloor that extends from Iceland south, ending near Antarctica), where magma continually spews out of the crack in the earth. The movement of these continental plates is what causes earthquakes to happen and mountains to form. Look at the shape of South America and compare it to the shape of West Africa. At one time, these two continents were connected.

I urge everyone to take some vacation time out west and witness firsthand God's created beauty in the mountains. There you will see rocks as big as skyscrapers sticking up out of the ground, being pushed by the Pacific plate sliding under the North American continental plate and lifting everything up. These rocks were almost melted by the heat under the continental crust, where they were bent and twisted (like warm taffy) as they were pushed up through the earth's crust, and now they dwell in plain view as an attraction for the many tourists passing by Cheyenne, Wyoming. I would like to recommend that the YECs do a little more research in the subject of geology.

"History is too short."

The following is a quotation from the Answers in Genesis web page: "According to evolutionists, Stone Age *Homo sapiens* existed for 190,000 years before beginning to make written records about four thousand to five thousand years ago. Prehistoric man built megalithic monuments, made beautiful cave paintings, and kept records of lunar phases. Why would early man wait two thousand centuries before using the same skills to record history? The biblical time scale is much more likely."[8]

As all historians know, history began with the invention of writing. Before the invention of writing, history, as we would call it, was passed down from generation to generation by repeated stories of legend and folklore, according to oral tradition, around the evening campfire. Obviously, in time the stories became elaborations of memory. We are referring to the time known as the Stone Age. By the early Stone Age (around 60,000 BC) humankind had developed a simple type of writing consisting simply of scratches or notches carved on a stick, a stone, or a bone. This is referred to as a "tally stick" because its purpose was to serve as a memory aid device. A person would make a scratch or notch for each of his possessions, such as sheep or cattle, or bushels of grain, or what was owed to him, or the battle that he won, or the enemies that he killed. The discovery of these "tally sticks" shows that the oldest profession was accounting. The idea of writing something that resembled a word, a thought, or an abstraction did not occur for many more centuries.

By the Neolithic era, part of the late Stone Age, around 6000 to 4000 BC, humankind added images to the idea of writing. It is possible to view these images (pictographs) scratched or painted on the walls of caves on the internet. I saw some of these ancient pictographs on a few of the cliffs in Monument Valley, Arizona, a few years back. The pictographs were used by the Stone Age humans to describe the game they hunted, where they found the animals, and the weapons they used to kill the game. At this point in the development of written communications, it was not possible to convey abstractions, such as the idea of love, with written words. But by using pictographs, humankind was able to convey the action of seeing something by painting an image of an eye, or the action of eating food by drawing a mouth, or the action of building a shelter by drawing a box or tent. Their writings as well as their thoughts were describing actual things, not abstractions, or ideas, or philosophy. Most paleographers estimate the date of the beginning of a written language to be simultaneous with the cuneiform script that was discovered in the diggings of ancient Sumer. The earliest cuneiform tablets found were dated to about 3500 BC. It is important to remember that the earliest writings were used mostly in commerce and personal communications.

The form of writing known as cuneiform was an attempt to simplify pictographic writings. Cuneiform script was formed by pressing a wedge-shaped stylus into soft clay, making various patterns that represented pictures or symbols and then baking the clay in order to harden and preserve it. Thousands of these cuneiform clay tablets have been found in the Middle East over the last few centuries, and we have learned a lot about the ancient cultures from them. The Egyptians developed their form of writing, known as hieroglyphic writing, around 3000 BC, which was also a combination of pictographic images and symbols. It may interest the reader to know that when Christopher Columbus landed in North America, almost none of the Native American tribes had a written language. Experts believe it was the Cherokee Nation that was the first to develop a written language on the American continent, but history clearly demonstrates that a written language came late in the life of most early civilizations.

Now let's get back to the issue of the AIG question, and that is, why didn't ancient humankind record history? First, according to the paleontologists, there was no written language in the Middle East before about 3500 BC. In addition, the early Hebrew language was very primitive. I doubt that Abraham spoke or wrote in the ancient Hebrew language. He probably knew and spoke in an ancient dialect of the Babylonian language that was the progenitor of the Hebrew language. That is part of my argument concerning the early book of Genesis. We believe that Moses may have written Genesis in an early Hebrew script, but we don't know for sure, because Moses and all the children of Israel lived in Egypt for four hundred years and they knew and spoke the Egyptian language. Much later, after Moses was gone and the nation of Israel was established, it is believed that scribes, trained in the Hebrew language of the time, translated Moses's writings, known as the Pentateuch, into the Hebrew language. That Hebrew is much older than the language in the book of Malachi (the last book of the Old Testament). There is a thousand-year gap between the Hebrew of Genesis and the Hebrew of Malachi, and we know that languages change greatly over time.

Second, ancient humankind did not see what we may call "history." To the ancients, life was nothing more than a cyclic struggle: that is, birth, death, day, night, feast, famine, winter, summer. The ancients believed that the purpose of life was to serve the gods from birth to death. This is what was taught in most ancient manuscripts. In the ancient world, it is difficult to find anyone who could legitimately be identified as a historian or journalist.

In the ancient Near East, events on earth were reflections of the activity of the gods.[9] The ancients did not report past events as history because to them everything that happened was believed to be judgments of the gods. It wasn't until the writings of Herodotus (a Greek historian, 484–425 BC) in the fifth century that any attempts were made to write a serious world history. Herodotus is often referred to as "the Father of History" because he was the first known historian to collect his materials systematically and critically and then arrange them into a *historical* narrative.

To conclude this issue about writing: it should interest the reader that the word for *write, writing,* or *written* (singular or plural), or any synonyms, occurs nowhere in the book of Genesis. It appears that when the early events of Genesis occurred, writing, as we accept it, had not been invented, and therefore Moses was not following a written text when he recorded the events found in the book of Genesis. Remember, many of the events described in the early chapters of Genesis occurred during what archeologists refer to as the late Stone Age.

"Noah's flood shaped Monument Valley and Devils Tower in Wyoming."

FIGURE 9.1 MONUMENT VALLEY   FIGURE 9.2 DEVILS TOWER

A few years ago I was watching a YouTube video produced by a young earth creationist (YEC). The subject of the video was the cause of the formation of the rock monoliths in Monument Valley, Arizona, and the Devils Tower, Wyoming. The argument proposed in the video was that both of these monoliths were created as a result of Noah's flood. Now by chance, I happened to have visited both of these fantastic features of the earth a few years earlier, and I had taken some photos of each. The YEC was desperately trying to prove that the earth was very young according to the YEC theology. His argument centered on the idea that both of these features were formed when Noah's floodwaters swept over the face of the earth so fast that they washed the soil away and left standing these giant rock monoliths. For the reader's information, the huge rock formations (monoliths) in Monument Valley and the Devils Tower reach upwards of eight hundred feet. They are just fantastic and almost unbelievable to see, so I took some pictures, which are displayed in figures 9.1 and 9.2. These monoliths are actually the cores of ancient volcanos, millions of years old. Erosion has removed the soft outer stone and soil and left only the hardened core formed by the earth's magma, flowing up from the mantle below in the form of lava.

Now I want the reader to notice something. If these monoliths were formed by the rushing water of Noah's flood, then there would be no debris surrounding these stone structures. The rushing floodwater would have swept the debris away. Instead, the rock debris is neatly piled around the base of these stone towers as if the debris just fell straight down due to gravity, wind, rain, and ice erosion. Well, that is exactly what happened. That YEC was trying to do something that many of his colleagues constantly try, and that is to come up with some explanation for the existence of phenomena because they refuse to accept an old earth scenario. The YEC failed to explain why these stone towers exist in the first place. The YECs will continually struggle to invent some make-believe science to critique all theories that suggest that the earth is older than six thousand years. I would like to add this idea for consideration: I recommend every reader of this book, sometime in their lives, to travel to the mountains of the western United States and view the fantastic scenery of our country. It is truly spectacular—and educational.

"Earth had a preflood vapor canopy."

Before we introduce this subject, we must first understand the scripture teaching underlying the problem.

> Then God said, "Let there be an expanse in the midst of the waters, and let it separate the waters from the waters." God made the expanse, and separated the *waters which were below* the expanse from the *waters which were above the expanse*; and it was so. *God called the expanse heaven.* And there was evening and there was morning, a second day. Then God said, "Let the waters below the heavens be gathered into one place, and let the dry land appear"; and it was so." (Genesis 1:6–9, emphasis added)

To sum up:

1. God created an expanse that He called heaven.
2. The expanse separated the waters, some of which were above the expanse, and some of which were below the expanse.
3. The waters below the expanse were gathered together so that the dry land would appear.

Now we covered this subject of the expanse in chapter 8. You may go back for a review. There we wrote the following: the King James Version of the Bible uses the word *firmament* as a translation in Genesis 1:6 for the word רקיע (pronounced as "ra-kee-a"). So the word *expanse* was chosen by the Lockman Foundation (translators of the *New American Standard Bible*) as a better translation of the Hebrew word *ra-kee-a* than the word *firmament*. English translators have had a problem with this word, as evidenced by the many different ways it has been translated into English. Just read some of the different English Bible translations and you will get the picture. In its essence, the word means something that is solid, impenetrable, such as a piece of metal flattened with a hammer, polished, and shaped like a bowl. The same idea appears in the Greek translation of Genesis where the Greek word means "something shaped like a bowl as if it were made from polished beaten metal." The image that the word implies is a metal object hammered into the shape of a bowl; then the bowl is placed upside down on top of our flat earth.[10] There it separates the waters above from the waters below. Notice that the text teaches that heaven is above the expanse, which is also translated as "the firmament," "the sky," "the space," or "a dome." Please note that the scriptures state that God separated the waters below the expanse (firmament) to become the rivers, lakes, and oceans.

I prefer the word *firmament* because it was chosen as the correct word for the Latin Vulgate (written in the fifth century), the principal Bible of the Middle Ages, and because it most closely identifies the physical barrier that God placed between the waters above and the waters below. Ancient cultures believed that there was a layer of water in the sky, above a solid crystal barrier, a translucent barrier. They believed this for two reasons:

1. because rain comes from the sky and
2. because the sky is blue, the color of water, and the translucent firmament allows the color blue to appear to all below.

Because the Hebrew nation, under the direction of Moses and the Lord, escaped from ancient Egypt, it stands to reason that they had accepted some of the Egyptian religious culture during their four hundred years of captivity and slavery in Egypt. The Egyptians (as well as many other civilizations of that era) also accepted an idea of a firmament that God had provided to hold up the rainwater. Notice in figure 7.2 in chapter 7 the Egyptian drawing of their idea/understanding of the cosmos. There you see the god Nut holding up the sky. This drawing, taken from Egyptian archives, confirms the popular but false idea of a "firmament" holding back the waters that existed as suggested in Genesis 1:14.

So based on the ancients' lack of knowledge concerning the nature of the earth and the atmosphere, it is understandable that they believed there was a barrier in the sky holding back the waters. It may be difficult for some to believe, but I have had occasion to meet some Christians in today's world who still believe that rain comes directly from the firmament in the sky. We find that idea taught in Genesis, where we read in verse 11 of chapter 7, "the floodgates of the sky were opened," and then in verse 2 of chapter 8, "the floodgates of the sky were closed, and the rain from the sky was restrained." Of course, the "floodgates" represent the access hatches in the firmament.

Now it stands to reason that if such a thing as the firmament existed, it would be impossible for NASA to send spaceships to the moon or, for that matter, even to put satellites in orbit around the earth, since the rockets would smash into the firmament and fall back to earth. By the way, I was listening to a lecture by a noted geologist recently, and he recounted his visit to the Creation Museum in Petersburg, Kentucky.[11] After entering the museum, he spotted a plaque on the wall that stated, "Reason Is the Enemy of Faith." That plaque sums up the basic issue with the YECs, which is that blind faith always wins over evidence and logic. The idea that reason is the enemy of faith is clearly a refutation of scripture where the Lord simply presents His case to a lost and dying world. Furthermore, that idea brings discredit on the Christian world.

"Water from above added to the flood."

About thirty-five years ago a gentleman named Joseph Dillow wrote a book entitled *The Waters Above*. In this book Mr. Dillow sought to prove that some of the waters that filled the earth during Noah's flood came from the upper atmosphere or, as he specified, from above the "firmament" (as found in the King James Version of the Bible). His argument, as stated in his book, implies that much of the water for Noah's flood came from the upper atmosphere, that is, above the firmament. He states, "This pre-flood atmosphere contained sufficient water vapor to sustain a 40 day and night rainfall of about 0.5 inches per hour. This amounts to about 40 feet of water and hence, 2.18 atmospheres of atmospheric pressure on the pre-flood earth."[12]

Let's think for a moment about Dillow's claim. He is correct when he claims that the atmospheric pressure would increase with all of this water in the upper atmosphere. He claims that the atmospheric pressure would increase to 2.18 times normal atmospheric pressure. The standard atmospheric pressure at sea level is 14.7 pounds per square inch on a normal day. If Mr. Dillow is correct, then before the flood, Adam and Eve and everyone else on earth would have had to suffer with an atmospheric pressure of 32.05 ($2.18 \times 14.7 = 32.05$) pounds on every square inch of their bodies. That kind of pressure would squash a person's lungs, making it difficult to breathe. It would also squash one's chest cavity and thereby affect the heart and blood pressure. A person's eyes would sink deeper into the skull. One's eardrums may rupture. The resulting problems (of which there are many) may result in the death of millions. I don't believe that Mr. Dillow knew what he was suggesting. His goal was to prove that his interpretation of the English Bible was the only correct interpretation, thereby reinforcing his view that the earth and universe is only a few thousand years old. He is wrong.

In the famous televised debate between Bill Nye and Ken Ham (referred to in chapter 5), where Bill Nye admitted that if Mr. Ham would show him *only one piece of evidence that the earth was young*, that is, less than ten thousand years, then he (Mr. Nye) would believe in a young earth. Mr. Ken Ham refused to provide any such evidence, perhaps because he didn't have any. I have provided ten factual items that clearly demonstrate that Answers in Genesis is wrong on their facts. Will they accept the truth and modify their teaching based on this presentation? I doubt it.

I trust the reader now understands why I wrote this chapter. It is because for too long the YECs have played fast and loose with known physical facts and data about our universe. They did this in order to convince the church crowds that their interpretation of the English Bible is the only correct interpretation and that every true Christian must agree that all creation was established by God on Sunday, October 23, 4004 BC. However, the evidence to the contrary is overwhelming! In this twenty-first century, attempts by the YECs to force their view onto the Christian community are helping to divide our churches and causing others to dismiss our faith. Let us now look at the next Biblical event that has been misinterpreted since the earliest times and has proven to be an embarrassment for the Christian Church.

[1] John Sailhamer, *Genesis Unbound* (Colorado Springs: Dawson Media, 2011), 35.

[2] G. Herbert Livingston, *The Pentateuch in Its Cultural Environment* (Grand Rapids, MI: Baker Book House, 1974), 148.

[3] Jonathan Sarfati, *Refuting Compromise* (Green Forest, AR: Master Books, 2004), 343.

[4] Source of "T-Rex picture, Hot Springs Country Pioneer Museum, Thermopolis, Wyoming

[5] https://answersingenesis.org/dinosaurs/when-did-dinosaurs-live/dinosaurs-eden.

[6] https://answersingenesis.org/astronomy/age-of-the-universe/evidence-for-a-young-world/.

[7] https://answersingenesis.org/geology/rock-layers/2-bent-rock-layers/

[8] Sarfati, *Refuting Compromise*, 284.

[9] John H. Walton, *Ancient Near Eastern Thought and the Old Testament* (Grand Rapids, MI: Baker Academic, 2006), 224.

[10] Merrill C. Tenney, ed., *The Zondervan Pictorial Encyclopedia of the Bible*, vol. 2 (Grand Rapids, MI: Zondervan, 1975), 540.

[11] David R. Montgomery, lecture on Noah's flood, Radcliffe Institute, Harvard University, April 9, 2015 (available on YouTube).

[12] Joseph Dillow, *The Waters Above* (Chicago: Moody Press, 1981), 137.

CHAPTER 10

Thoughts about the Genesis Flood

The purpose of this chapter is to examine the scriptural claims concerning details of the Genesis flood. I believe that much of the common interpretations of this flood passage are the result of the presuppositions of the church passed down through the centuries. I believe that the text of scripture clearly proclaims that the universal flood covered only the known ancient world at that time, not the entire earth (the third planet from the sun).

We accept the claim that Moses was the author of the first five books of the Bible (also known as the Pentateuch, or the Torah—i.e., Genesis, Exodus, Leviticus, Numbers, and Deuteronomy). This claim is asserted in many other verses of scripture (Mark 12:26, Luke 24:44, and John 9:29 are examples). The Exodus of the people of Israel from Egypt is dated to about 1400 BC. Moses led the people from captivity in Egypt to wanderings in the wilderness of Sinai for forty years. It is commonly assumed that Moses wrote the history of the world and the accounts of the children of Abraham during this period, which has been passed down to us in the book of Genesis. The events in the book of Genesis predated Moses by many years. We know this because the children of Abraham were captive in Egypt for about four hundred years (Genesis 15:13). Therefore, Moses did not have firsthand knowledge of any of the events of and accounts in the book of Genesis.

All of this is said to affirm to the reader that Moses (under the guidance of the Holy Spirit) wrote the history of the world in Genesis from memory of tales told to him, from folklore, using knowledge common among the

Hebrew people and the rest of the civilized world, using some information from God, and perhaps from accessing some written sources. We do not know and we may never know exactly how Moses was informed or was taught the history of Abraham and his children or the world history that preceded Abraham. However, one thing we can be sure of is that Moses did not write a scientific treatise of the universe.

Moses wrote according to the accepted knowledge of his day. The ancients believed that the earth was flat and that it was covered by the heavens and water (Genesis 1:6–7) through a separation known as the firmament (the *New American Standard Bible* translates the word as "expanse"). It was this firmament that kept rainwater from falling to earth, and it was the firmament that had the windows of heaven that were opened on occasion to let rainwater fall to the ground below (see Genesis 7:11, "floodgates of the sky"). Therefore it is imperative to interpret the account of the early earth from the viewpoint of the ancients, as well as those accounts from the days before Abraham and Noah.

In Genesis 6–8, the word *earth* (*erets*, ארץ) is found thirty-seven times, and the word *land* (*adama*, אדמה) occurs six times. Somewhere in past Christian thinking, the word *earth* came to mean the whole of planet Earth, that giant sphere that obits the sun. Also, the word *land* came to mean essentially all the land under the sky (or heavens). These interpretations constitute a serious error. For the definitions of these words, I made reference to the popular Hebrew lexicon by Francis Brown, S. R. Driver, and C. A. Briggs.[1] According to this lexicon, these words appear to be almost be synonyms, as their definitions are very similar. For the word *adama*, the most common definitions were "land," "ground," "country," "dirt," and "soil." I would like to point out that the word for "man" is *adam*, meaning "dirt" or "dust," which is what God used to make humankind (Genesis 2:7). When reading the first four or five chapters of Genesis, it is difficult to determine when God is referring to humankind, human beings, or to the first man, Adam. The translators will usually capitalize the word *Adam* when they want the reader to understand that the text is referring to the first man by name. But you must understand, this is strictly the opinion of the translators. The question that still remains is, did God create Adam (*adam*) or humanity (*adam*), or both? We believe He created both, but we cannot be certain of the time or date from the text of scripture.

For the word *erets*, the most common definition given was "earth, country, dust, ground, floor, land, territories, world, inhabited lands, etc." Now I want the reader to understand that nowhere in scripture are these words used to refer to our planet, the third rock from the sun. Some will argue that if the scripture uses the adjective *whole* or *all* with the word *erets*, the text must mean the whole physical earth or the planet. Let's stop and look at a few other verses before we jump to conclusions. When we read Genesis 41:56–57, we see the use of the word *all* when it doesn't truly mean "all." Please refer to my comments in chapter 5 concerning these verses.

Look at the use of the word *all*. Does this scripture indicate that there was famine in the land known today as the British Isles? In South Africa? In South America? In China? In Canada? In Alaska? Of course not. The use of the word *all* is what is known as a figure of speech called a hyperbole, or exaggeration for the purpose of emphasizing an important point. The point was simply that there would be a serious drought over some of the Middle East countries, leaving these nations short of food, and famine was the result. Let's look at another example, in Daniel 2:39: "After you there will arise another kingdom inferior to you, then another third kingdom of bronze, which will rule over *all* the earth."

This text is from the response of Daniel to King Nebuchadnezzar of Babylon. Here Daniel is explaining the prophecy that another kingdom will replace Babylon (the Medes and Persians, fulfilled in 538 BC) and that this new kingdom will rule over *all the earth* (hyperbole—it actually means over all the inhabited or known earth, not our planet). There are many more examples like this in the Bible, but for now, I believe that the point has been made that we must consider the manner and type of speech before we determine an exact meaning.

When God tells Noah of the impending flood, He says, "I am bringing the flood of water upon the *earth*, to destroy *all* flesh in which is the breath of life, from under heaven; *everything* that is on the *earth* shall perish" (Genesis 6:17, emphasis added). Does this verse express hyperbole? I believe it does. The meaning is clear: God was going to destroy all life in His designated area, not in Asia, Africa, or North and South America. To get an idea of the area that God was referring to, just look at the Table of Nations in Genesis 10. Moses wrote Genesis, and this Table of Nations represents the nations that Moses was aware of at the time of his writing. Remember, this Table of Nations includes nations that arose after the flood, but notice that all of these nations are located in what we refer to as the Middle East, not the rest of planet Earth. Therefore, according to scripture, there was no reason for God to destroy the rest of the world if it was uninhabited or believed not to exist. Moses was not aware of the North American continant, nor the millions of Natives living there. Neither was he aware of South America, Alaska, Australia, China, and so forth.

The scripture tells us that it was God's plan to destroy all flesh by means of the flood because of the rampant evil afflicting humankind. Scripture also tells us that part of the problem with the moral state of humankind was the Nephilim (the giants resulting from the immoral union between the sons of God and the daughters of men). It is important to note that the Nephilim were not totally destroyed by the flood, because we read in Numbers 13:33 that they were still in the land of Canaan, which Israel was planning to conquer. So the flood did not destroy all flesh. Correctly understanding Genesis takes more than a casual reading of the English text.

God told Noah that He would spare him and his family by having him build a vessel in which he and his family could survive while God poured out His judgement on the rest of the humans on the earth. God gave the dimensions of the vessel or ark to Noah. Based on what we read in the Bible, we understand that the ark was to be about 450 feet long and about 45 feet wide. We do not know the date of the flood, but we can speculate that it occurred before 3500 BC. See the source mentioned in note number 4, listed at the end of this chapter, for more information. This time period was before the development of iron (about 1200 BC), so Noah would not have been able to use iron straps, nails, or bolts to hold the wooden boat together. As a point of general information, the largest wooden boat ever built by the Roman Empire (about AD 250) was about 180 feet. It could not be any longer because the wood was not strong enough to hold the whole thing together, even though the Romans used iron straps and nails to fasten the planks of wood siding to the vessel's frame and bulkheads, thereby holding the whole thing together.

By the eighteenth century, the British Empire was able to build one of their famous man-of-war ships to a length of 350 feet. That was the largest wooden warship ever built by human beings up to that time, as recorded in common history. The British just could not build it any bigger, even though they were able to use iron nails, bolts, screws, and straps. The bending and torsional stress on the wooden frame would have caused the wooden bulkheads and the hull structure to collapse. Other large wooden boats were built, some by the American ship yards in the early 20th century, but all were failures because wood was not stiff enough to hold together even with iron bolts and iron strapping.

It was with the application of iron for the ship's structure, including the hull, at the end of the nineteenth century that ships could be built bigger than 350 feet. So the question lingers, how did Noah hold the wooden ship frame and bulkheads together? We are not told. I believe that God can perform any miracle He so chooses, but there is no mention of a miracle in the building of the ark. So again, we are left with a dilemma: God miraculously held the timbers of the ark together, or we are seeing another example of hyperbole, or some early copyist got it wrong when recording the length of the ark from an early manuscript (mistakes like this have happened before).

Another problem is that we know the ark was made from gopher wood, but no one knows anything about gopher wood. Nowhere in the Bible is gopher wood identified. In addition, the Mesopotamian plain, where Noah lived, is known for its scarcity of wood. So where did Noah get all the wood required to build the ark? We also know that the ark was about 450 feet long. This means that the gopher wood had to be cut from trees that were 450 feet tall, or else there had to be a method of joining planks of gopher wood together to make them 450 feet long so that the planks could cover the total length of the ark. We have already mentioned that there were no metals available prior to about 3000 BC from which Noah could make nails or straps or something else to hold the planks together or to attach the planks to the keel or the chine or the bulkheads. In addition, the planks of gopher wood had to have been sawn from logs of gopher wood, but you need strong metals from which to make the saw blades. Since iron was not discovered until about 1500 BC and not mined and smelted until about 1200 BC, Noah could not have made metal saws from iron. If the ark was made before about 3500 BC. Noah would not even have had brass or bronze from which to make saws.

Further, bronze is hardened brass (by adding a small amount of tin), but bronze is not strong enough to make a ripping saw, which is needed to make sheathing planks for the ark. A bronze saw might make it through one log, but it would need to be sharpened again and again until there would be no saw teeth left on the saw blade. Since we can't be certain of the dates of the flood, all we can guess is that Noah lived during the late Stone Age or the very early Bronze Age (3500 BC). Could Noah have built the ark using stone tools? Very doubtful! Could Noah have built the ark using early brass or bronze tools? Very difficult!

Throughout the centuries, as the Bible was explained to the churches, it was understood that the Genesis flood covered all the earth including the mountains, according to Genesis 7:19–20 and 8:5. Most people presumed that this verse implies that the highest mountains on earth are included. When Mount Everest was discovered, the church readily accepted that the flood had to be high enough to cover Mount Everest, or else the flood had to have reached a depth of at least twenty-nine thousand feet above sea level. We need to make a point concerning this conclusion. If anyone would care to check, one would discover that the Hebrew word (Old Testament) for "mountain" and the Hebrew word for "hill" are exactly the same. The word in the Old Testament translated "mountain" is *har* (הר), and the word translated "hill" is exactly the same word. How can you tell the difference? Without the context, you can't.

In Genesis 7:19, the author added the adjective *high* before the word *mountain*, thereby indicating that the landform was larger than a simple hill. But these words still do not give enough information for us to declare that the water was deeper than the average mountains were high. The earliest known recorded civilizations on planet Earth were located in the Mesopotamian valley between the Euphrates and Tigris Rivers. The Bible seems to imply that the flood of Genesis occurred there. According to geologists, there is a large layer of flood silt located there to indicate that it is the actual site of a gigantic flood.[2] The following quotation from the book *Ancient Civilizations*, by Hayes and Hanscom, is very informative on this subject:

> About 4000 B.C. an especially frightful calamity occurred. The entire delta plain was swept by a river

flood so great that it left a bed of clay eight feet thick over the countryside. Farms, villages, animals, men, perished except in the two or three towns that stood on the highest mounds. The discovery in 1929 of evidence of this flood was of great interest to Bible students. It gave some substance to the legend of Noah and the Ark, a legend already known to duplicate in many details a Mesopotamian legend of a world flood.[3]

It is interesting to note that the oldest known continuously occupied city in the world is Jericho, located near the Dead Sea, next to the mountains of Israel. The city has been occupied for at least seven thousand to eight thousand years (this is a proven fact that can be examined by any interested party). Despite intense archeological diggings over many years, no evidence of a destruction of Jericho by a flood exists.[4] This lack of evidence indicates that the flood was not universal, since the city of Jericho was untouched.

For those who teach that the earth and all creation is but a mere six thousand years old, it is interesting to discover the word *pitch* in the text of the Old Testament. In Genesis 6:14—"Make for yourself an ark of gopher wood; you shall make the ark with rooms, and shall cover it inside and out with *pitch*" (emphasis added)—this word is used to describe a black gooey substance that oozes up from the ground. It was considered a curse by the gods because it ruined the soil for agricultural pursuits. In those days, pitch was readily available in the southern Mesopotamian valley (ancient Babylon). The original word is *copher* (כפר), and according to the *Hebrew and English Lexicon*, the root word means "to cover." A literal translation of Genesis 6:14 would be "thou shall pitch it with pitch." The verb form of the word means "to cover" or "to smear." The noun form of the word means a black, sticky, gooey substance that oozes up from the ground. So the ark was to be covered inside and outside with this stuff. What was this stuff? This pitch was tar, bitumen—a petroleum product from the fossil remains of the ancient world of dinosaurs, jungle foliage, vegetation, and other living stuff that has decayed underground over millions of years into a biomass, which is now harvested by the modern Arab nations as *oil!* And we refine it and then burn it in our automobiles as gasoline. It's a gift from God. Hallelujah! The pitch was not used to hold the gopher wood logs together, but it was used to waterproof and seal the final assembly so that the ark would not leak.

In these chapters about the flood, we have several verses that appear to be contradictions. Notice the following verse, Genesis 8:7: "And he sent out a raven, and it flew here and there until the water was dried up from the *earth*" (emphasis added). (Note: The raven flew around until the water was gone. There was no need to send out the dove.)

Next, compare Genesis. 8:5 with Genesis 8:9:

- "The water decreased steadily until the tenth month; in the tenth month, on the first day of the month, the tops of the mountains *became visible*" (Genesis 8:5, emphasis added).
- "Then he sent out a dove from him, to see if the water was abated from the face of the *land*; but the dove found no resting place for the sole of her foot, so she returned to him into the ark, for the water was on the *surface of all the earth*" (Genesis 8:8–9, emphasis added).

Read Genesis 7:19–20 and see what it says about the mountains. The mountains were covered with the flood, yet the mountains were visible. Notice the phrase "the dove found no resting place for the sole of her foot." Notice that verse 5 says that the tops of the mountains (hills) were visible. Because of the curvature of the earth, it is not possible to see much farther than twenty to thirty miles. This fact means that Noah could see the mountaintops in the distance and the dove could easily fly to those mountaintops within thirty to forty-five minutes. The dove could have easily found a resting place after a short flight.

Is there a contradiction in the Word of God? No, because the Genesis story is incomplete and does not contain enough information for us to make a correct evaluation. Simply stated, the flood account in Genesis is not detailed sufficiently so that the modern reader may form solid conclusions. We must accept what is written as a general outline, and we must not expect to garner great detail from the account in the Bible. The message of the flood is not about the history of the earth and creation, but instead about God's judgment of sin. Therefore we must not read Genesis

6–8 anticipating an accurate lesson on earth's geology. This is exactly what the YECs do. They continually suggest that all geological features on the face of the earth are direct results of Noah's flood.

Another subject of interest concerning the flood narrative is that the ark is not referred to as a boat or ship, even though its purpose was to rescue some from death through the epic-making flood. The Hebrew word for "ark" in Genesis is *tay-vath* (תבת). This word is used twenty-eight times between Genesis 6:14 and Exodus 2:5. It appears in the feminine form in the text, and it means "box, chest, vessel, basket, coffin, or coffer," according to BDB lexicon.[5] This definition is also confirmed in the *Hebrew–Chaldee Lexicon* by Gesenius.[6] In the Greek translation of the Old Testament, known as the Septuagint, the Hebrew scholars of the second century BC translated the Hebrew word as *kebooton* (κιβωτον), which means "box, chest, coffin."[7] The English word *ark* comes from the Latin *arca*, meaning "coffin, box, cell, chest, coffer, and place of imprisonment."

The *Oxford English Dictionary* defines the English word *ark* as a "chest, box, basket, coffin, or a coffer." The word first appeared in English literature about the thirteenth or fourteenth century. An example provided by the dictionary is a quotation from Claxton (AD 1475), from an article titled "Jason," where it reads, *"That thou go into pyre [forest] for to make an arke"*[8] (67; emphasis added). The very first published English translation of the Hebrew Old Testament was by Coverdale, AD 1535. In this publication, Coverdale chose to use the Latin word for "box" or "chest" to translate the Hebrew word *tay-vath* (תבת). His translation reads, "Make thee an ark of pyne tre [pine tree] and make chambers in it and pitch it within and without with pitch and make it after this fashion."

So Coverdale correctly understood the meaning of the Hebrew word and the equivalent translation in the Latin Vulgate (the current Bible for the past one thousand years of Western civilization). Since then, every English Bible has used the word *ark*. It is important to note that Coverdale did not translate the Hebrew word as "boat" or "ship", yet most all readers of our modern versions interpret the word *ark* to mean just that: a boat or ship.

The land on which Noah lived was in the Mesopotamian valley, between the Tigris and Euphrates rivers where most people made their living fishing in the river waters. This fact means that most everyone has access to boats. When the flood came, many could have retreated to their boats and survived.

If the Hebrew writers had wanted to identify the vessel that rescued Noah and his family as a boat or ship, they would have used the correct Hebrew word, which is *a-nee-ah* (אניה).[9] Since the original writer of Genesis did not use the Hebrew word for "boat" or "ship," why would we assume that is what he meant by using the Hebrew word meaning "box, chest, coffin, vessel, or basket"? After a careful study of the description of Noah's ark, I believe it looked more like a very large Mississippi River barge. There is a Christian organization in Williamstown, Kentucky, that has constructed a replica of their idea of Noah's ark. It looks like a large seagoing vessel, only needing sail or engine to navigate the biggest oceans. Actually their image is far from the concept derived from a careful reading of scripture. The purpose of the ark was to rescue Noah and his family, plus other living creatures (as God had selected), from death by drowning in the coming flood. The ark was not intended to navigate the oceans or to transport Noah and his family from one place to another.

One other point of interest: Noah was to rescue two of every kind of animal from death by the flood as God had directed. However, an item that is not too well-known is that about 99 percent of all animal life that ever lived on earth is extinct. If the flood occurred about four thousand years ago (for the sake of discussion), most of the animals that lived prior to the flood ceased to exist. So Noah failed in his assignment to rescue all the animals.

In conclusion, I wrote this chapter to suggest that we have an inspired Word from God, but that this Word, the Bible, does not include enough information to answer all our questions or to explain everything we would wish to know about creation. We must accept that the Bible is infallible in all that it affirms, but that it is not always accurate concerning matters of geology, biology, cosmology and other areas of actual modern science, because God did not intend to lecture the ancients on the fundamentals of modern science. We must accept that God had to have written His Word in a language and cultural style that His intended audience could understand. That means He had to accommodate their ignorance of today's knowledge of science and the universe. Further, we must accept what it says as that which God desires us to know about His creation, but we must not force a twenty-first-century interpretation on everything it says. We do not have a simple method of interpretation. Our efforts of interpretation must be based on careful study, knowing that we are reading a manuscript that reflects an ancient culture of which we are not fully cognizant. We must never try to interpret the Bible according to our modern principles and traditions. Therefore, study it intently and carefully.

[1] Francis Brown, S. R. Driver, and C. A. Briggs, *The Hebrew and English Lexicon of the Old Testament* (Oxford: Clarendon Press, 1978).

[2] John Walton, ed., *Zondervan Illustrated Bible Backgrounds Commentary*, vol. 1 (Grand Rapids, MI: Zondervan, 2009), 50.

[3] Carlton J. H. Hayes and J. Hanscom, *Ancient Civilizations* (New York: Macmillan, 1968), 58.

[4] Walton, *Zondervan*, 50.

[5] Brown, Driver, and Briggs, *The Hebrew and English Lexicon*, 1061c.

[6] S. P. Tregelles, *Gesenius Hebrew–Chaldee Lexicon to the Old Testament* (Grand Rapids, MI: Eerdmans, 1978), 855a.

[7] H. G. Liddell and R. Scott, *Greek–English Lexicon* (Oxford: Clarendon Press, 1978), 950.

[8] *Oxford English Dictionary*, vol. 1 (Oxford: Oxford University Press, 1979), 448.

[9] This word is described in Zondervan's *Strongest NASB Exhaustive Concordance* (1998), 1363, #591.

CHAPTER 11

A Discussion on Biological Evolution

The principal reason that young earth creationists (YECs) do not want to interpret Genesis any other way than as describing a literal six days of creation a mere six thousand years ago is simply that they believe in evolution. The YECs believe that if they agree that the evidence clearly shows an old earth creation, then the concept of biological evolution must be true, since it has been stated many times that evolution takes millions, if not billions, of years. So let's examine this point a little more closely. What if the idea of *random biological evolution* as proclaimed by Charles Darwin and most scientists is *not correct*, countering the claims of the modern scientific community? I personally believe that God created everything that now exists or has ever existed. However, when I see the remains of the ancient animals such as dinosaurs, and when I have examined the archeologists' claims that these creatures existed millions of years ago, their conclusions being based on irrefutable evidence that I have studied, I have but one possible conclusion, and that is to accept that these creatures lived a very long time ago.

I picked up some samples of ancient life-forms while I was visiting the fossil digs in the mountains of Wyoming, and I kept these fossils in my study just to remind me that they are real. So as far as I can see, the age of T. rex is over sixty million years, and there is nothing I can do to change that fact. I have also picked up some stone-encapsulated fossils on the beaches of Florida, just next to Tampa Bay, and have added them to my collection. So the problem is this: my eyes have not deceived me, and neither has my education in advanced physics and mathematics. In fact, if the reader spent more time walking outdoors, always looking down, examining every odd geological feature that came into view, the reader would find a lot of evidence to back up my conclusions.

Only a few years ago a farmer near Chelsea, Michigan, was walking his fields when he stumbled upon a white object sticking out of the ground. After he dug up this object, it was determined that it was a leg bone from an ancient wooly mammoth. Scientists from the University of Michigan formed a team and collected the complete skeleton for study. It is now being prepared for display in the University of Michigan's Museum of Natural History. Following multiple tests, the age of the mammoth was determined to be greater than fifteen thousand years. So the conclusion is, be careful when digging in your backyard, because you just may find some evidence of ancient life-forms that prove the earth is older than six thousand years.

Here are the questions that I wish to address: What if God chose to use a procedure or process that we don't understand to create life? Was the creation of the animals in Genesis 1:4–5 an instantaneous miracle, or was more time involved? Remember, we discussed the meaning of "days" of creation in chapter 5 and the first two chapters of Genesis in chapter 8 of *And There Was Light*. I have concluded, based on the text of scripture and many notable theologians whom I quoted, that these six days mentioned in Genesis are not twenty-four hours each. The ancient mind-set was not cognizant of time as we are. If you were to ask an ancient Hebrew (just set free from Egypt) how old he was, he couldn't answer you, except to add that he was born during the reign of some king or prophet. The ancient mind was centered on daily life. He got up at dawn and he went to bed at dusk. Life was just a daily cycle. The Egyptians kept track of months and years, but early on their methods were not very accurate. It was not necessary for God to tell these ancients exactly when and how He created everything, because they were not thinking about it. It was only necessary to tell them that He, God Almighty, the God of Abraham, created everything.

Next consider this: Is God required to tell us how He created life? If God told us how He created life, would we understand? Now think about this idea: perhaps God chose to create life in stages, over millions of years. Is there any biblical proof otherwise? Look at Genesis 1:12, where it says,

"Let the earth sprout vegetation." Now God created it, but the scriptures say that the vegetation came from the earth. Therefore the scripture implies that God created the vegetation, but He used the earth to do it.

By creating vegetable matter (grasses and trees and other foliage) hundreds of millions of years ago, God created our coal and oil deposits. By creating the animal life like the dinosaurs, insects, and fish, and then destroying many of them millions of years ago (in the Permian extinction about 250 million years ago, and then in the Cretaceous extinction about 65 million years ago), God created our gas and more oil deposits. All these things God created for the benefit for His last and greatest creation, mankind. Let's add one more idea to our thinking: What if God created bipedal humanlike beings to populate the earth in order to do His bidding in the final stages of creation? Is God required to tell us about these things in His Bible? I don't believe so. We do know for certain that modern humankind, for a period of time, shared the earth with a race of humanlike creatures called the Neanderthal. Don't bother arguing with the facts. At present, there exist hundreds of skeletons of Neanderthals in museums around the world, and it is possible to go and view them. That is a fact that the YECs have a hard time dealing with. We need to be thankful for what God has told us.

The physical evidence in the rocks seems to confirm the idea of a progressive creation, created and layered in stages. One of the most important concepts that one will learn while studying geology (or earth science) is the proven idea of the "stratigraphic column." Every geology book has an explanation and drawings of this concept, as it is very important to understand if one expects to understand the natural world. The surface of the earth is constantly changing. Wind, rain, snow, ice, gravity, and earthquakes all work together to rearrange the ground around us, but it takes time before we humans notice any changes. When things die, such as wildlife, trees, leaves, and other foliage, an additional layer on earth is formed by these things. As an example, I live on land that is about eight feet above the bottom of the old Lake Erie. Today the Lake Erie shoreline is about twenty miles east of my property, but many centuries ago my property was at the bottom of Lake Erie.

I know these things to be a fact, because ten years ago I was appointed by the township to oversee the installation of a sewer system on my road, and while the backhoe operator was digging I noticed a level of white gravel about eight feet below the surface of my front yard. I asked the backhoe operator to bring up some of that white stuff so that I could examine it. To my surprise, when I looked at the fine white gravel through an eye loupe, I discovered that each tiny piece of that supposed gravel was actually a very small seashell, about one-eighth of an inch in size. The backhoe operator later said that he finds the same stuff all over this corner of southern Michigan. He concluded that I was looking at the bottom of Lake Erie as it was thousands of years ago. Those little seashells are now part of the stratigraphic column.

I am writing this to illustrate the idea that the earth beneath our feet is made up of stuff that has collected over many, many years. As time passes, the ground beneath our feet collects a record of the past; the oldest items are at the bottom of the soil, and the most recent items are near the top. This natural process is called "stratification." You can see examples of stratification as you travel along I-75 through Kentucky and Tennessee. Just stop and examine the road-cuts, where you will see the strata lines in the stone. You will see the same lines along the cliffs bordering Lake Michigan near Petoskey and Charlevoix, Michigan. As one travels out west, one is greeted by miles of stone cliffs with very prevalent strata lines. Each of these strata lines is proof of the old age of the earth, simply because you can stop and see the fossil evidence in them. To conclude, a stratigraphic column contains a sequential historical record of the past, the oldest material (sedimentary rocks and fossils) at the bottom of the rock layers and the youngest material at the top. Many years ago, scientist discovered that dinosaur bones were located way down in the geologic column and humanlike bones were right near the top, so humans and dinosaurs did not live together.

All of this is mentioned to help the reader understand that the dating of rocks and fossils can be very accurate if one understands the geologic column. So when an explorer finds bones that are very similar to a human skeleton, yet not the same as those of a modern human ask yourself these questions: What should the explorer believe? Should he go to the Bible to discover the principles of geology? Do you, the reader, see the problem? God never intended us to use His Word as a textbook on geology. So what are we to do with skeleton bones that look somewhat similar to those of a modern human, but not exactly, and not the same as those of any other creature on earth? This is the problem that modern YECs fail to address. From the evidence, it appears that God in His wisdom created humanlike beings (humanoids) sometime in the very ancient past, and He chose not to tell us about these things in His Bible. One possible exception that stands out are the following questions: Who was Cain afraid of? Who did Cain marry? Who populated the city that Cain built (Genesis 4:14–17)? These verses clearly indicate that there existed other humanlike beings in the days of Cain.

Now the question that we first brought up is, Did God create humankind and all other animals through the process called biological (Darwinian) evolution? My answer is, I don't know, and neither does anyone else. However, I find a serious problem with Darwinian evolution, namely, the idea of randomness. The idea of random evolution puts God out of the creation. I refuse to accept that idea, simply because in all of creation, we clearly see the work of a designer. That negates "randomness." A fundamental concept of logic is that *chaos does not produce order.* If order is to come from chaos, then there must be an intelligence that engineers the order.

The Bible begins with the statement in Genesis 1:2 "without form and empty." This is my translation of the Hebrew text "תהו ובהו (tohu wa-bohu)." The first word literally means "formlessness, confusion," and the second word literally means "emptiness." This phrase is a simple expression of the chaos that existed when God created all matter and energy and then brought all of it into existence at once (this fits neatly into the big bang scenario). Simply stated, the beginning was all chaos. The rest of Genesis 1 describes God creating order from the chaos. After each creative act, God said it was "good." The word *good* in this context simply means that all that He created now fits into His intended order. The word *good* was not in reference to a lack of sin as many YECs imply.

I personally hold to the idea of a divine designer because it best fits the data, both biblical and biological. This can be a subject of another book, but there are some excellent books already available that cover this subject of design in great detail. I heartily recommend the following two books that I have carefully read: *The Creator and the Cosmos* by Hugh Ross (NavPress, 2005) and *Is God a Mathematician?* by Mario Livio (Simon & Schuster, 2009).

Both of these books demonstrate, with the evidence available in the universe, that there is a designer behind our creation. Mario Livio quotes the British physicist James Jeans (1877–1946), who once said, "The universe appears to have been designed by a pure mathematician."

The following are comments concerning biological creation and evolution from a purely random chance scenario. The conclusion is that the concept is impossible.

Murray Eden, in his article "Heresy in the Halls of Biology," wrote, "It is our contention that if 'random' is given a serious and crucial interpretation from a probabilistic point of view, the randomness postulate is highly implausible and that an adequate scientific theory of evolution must await the discovery and elucidation of new natural laws."[1]

Sir Fred Hoyle, a prominent astronomer and cosmologist of the twentieth century, and a onetime atheist, said that evolution is comparable with the chance that "a tornado sweeping through a junk-yard might assemble a Boeing 747 from the materials therein."[2]

Sir Hoyle added the following later in his article:

> The trouble is that there are about two thousand enzymes for life to exist, and the chance of obtaining them all in a random trial is only one part in $(10^{20})^{2,000} = 10^{40,000}$ Any theory with a probability of being correct that is larger than one part in $10^{40,000}$ must be judged superior to random shuffling [of evolution]. The theory that life was assembled by intelligence has, we believe, a probability vastly higher than one part in $10^{40,000}$ of being the correct explanation of the many curious facts discussed in preceding chapters. Indeed, such a theory is so obvious that one wonders why it is not widely accepted as being self-evident. The reasons are psychological rather than scientific.[3]

Before I close this chapter, I must add the following conclusions of Dr. Stephen Hawking, a world-famous astronomer and cosmologist for his work on black holes, and also a noted atheist. In chapter 8 of his book *A Brief History of Time*, where he discusses the origin of the universe, he writes, "The whole history of science has been the gradual realization that events do not happen in an arbitrary manner, but that they reflect a certain underlying order, which may or may not be divinely inspired."[4] Then he adds, "It would be very difficult to explain why the universe should have begun in just this way, except as an act of a God who intended to create beings like us."[5]

It is interesting to consider that since the beginning of humankind, no new species of animals or humankind have been created; however, many have ceased to exist. Also, there has been no change in the human DNA for at least the last ten thousand years. Most archeologists agree that modern civilized humankind appeared on earth about that time. So biological evolution, if there ever was such a thing, seems to have stopped, because no new forms of species have been detected and the DNA remains the same. Let me conclude with this idea: God created everything, but He didn't tell us enough about His procedure so that we might be able to understand it. Is there anything wrong with this idea, theologically speaking? It is still God who gets the credit and glory, and humankind who receives the riches.

[1] Murray Eden, "Heresy in the Halls of Biology: Mathematicians Question Darwinism," *Scientific Research* (November 1967): 64.
[2] Fred Hoyle, "Hoyle on Evolution," *Nature* 29 (November 12, 1981): 105.
[3] Hoyle, 130.
[4] Stephen Hawking, *A Brief History of Time* (New York: Bantam Books, 1996), 157.
[5] Hawking, 163.

CHAPTER 12

My Quest and Conclusion

I must begin with my presupposition that a creator is responsible for all that exists. I choose to acknowledge my belief system as the only possible answer to the question of origins, namely that the God of the Hebrew Scriptures, the God of Abraham, Isaac, and Jacob (and the one who took on a body of flesh and dwelt among us, according to John 1:14), is the Creator. Logic tells us that if anything now exists, then something had to have caused it. In other words, there has to be something that is eternal and external. Modern science has clearly discovered and proven that the universe has not always existed. Therefore the universe is not eternal, because it had a beginning. And because of this, something must have created it, because it did not create itself. No other explanation will work. That which is eternal is God Almighty who revealed Himself to Abraham. And God must be external because He is not part of the universe that He created. Instead He dwells in, on, above, around, and outside His creation. God was not created. He is both eternal and external. This I take as my basic presupposition and by faith.

Some consider that the Bible is full of recorded miracles, but it is not. Miracles were permitted by God generally during important periods in Israel's history, such as the formation of the nation of Israel, as warnings of coming judgment; by Jesus to authenticate His claim of being the expected Messiah; and during the formation of the early church. So in the final analysis, miracles were not the normative practice throughout scripture. I believe this was for a very important reason, namely that God has clearly said in the book of Hebrews, "Without faith it is impossible to please Him" (Hebrews 11:6). Had God wanted to convert the whole world, He most likely would have arranged for continuous miracles over all the centuries since Abraham. I see faith as the only avenue by which one can come to Almighty God. Remember, Jesus performed some fantastic miracles (like the raising of Lazarus from the dead—John 11:43), yet some of the witnesses still wanted to kill him, and Lazarus also (John 11:53). So the conclusion is that miracles do not always convince the unbelievers. This is one of the reasons that I have little patience with those who try to prove God's existence. This idea removes faith from God's equation.

When we are considering the creation of the universe, some would consider that it was a miracle. Modern science has shown that all that exists, the universe and all that is in it, was created from nothing (in less time than required to blink an eye), as told us in Hebrews 11:3: "By faith we understand that the worlds were prepared by the word of God, so that what is seen was not made out of things which are visible."

Was creation a miracle, or was it only God rearranging the order of the invisible particles of space to produce everything? I don't know, and I believe that no one else knows either. If I were planning on writing a science textbook, I would go into much greater detail, but I'm afraid that such a thing would not be appropriate for the scope of *And There Was Light*.

When we examine the universe closely, we discover many strange and amazing things that we do not understand, and that we may never understand, but the Creator may have used unheard-of science to create all that exists. Can we call it a miracle? Perhaps. A study on modern physics reveals many strange things, such as quantum entanglement, special relativity of space and time, the substance of electromagnetic radiation, the strong nuclear force, and the substance of gravity—and much, much more. These are things that modern humankind can use in the development of knowledge and the progress of science, but we still don't understand what they are. No one knows. So the universe is full of mysteries, but can we refer to these things as miracles? Do you see where I am going with this line of reasoning? These natural phenomena, which fill our world, have led many in the past to refer to them as "miracles." So as you see, the problem lies in the matter of definition. What is the difference between a miracle and a natural, unexplained, not-understood phenomenon? I believe God works according to the laws of His creation, even if we do not understand. An additional idea requires us to ask ourselves, what is the difference between a miracle that takes one second to accomplish and one that takes millions of years? Is an event less of a miracle because it took time to see its creation? If it took billions of years for God to accomplish the creation of the universe as we now see it, can we consider this as evidence that creation is not a miracle? I think not.

Whatever process God used to create all that exists, we may never know. I wasn't there to see it, and neither were you, so we must accept this fact of creation by faith. The atheist has a problem when he or she tries to explain why, when nothing preexisted, something came into existence from nothing, by itself. Many scientists and philosophers are still grappling with this problem.

But there exists an even more serious problem for the Christian church, and that is the force that some in the fundamentalist class of Christian churches use to insist that all true believers must accept God's creation as having taken place on October 23, 4004 BC. This concept is driving too many people away from the gospel and the church. The young earth creationists that call me names such as "Christian atheist" and "false teacher" are doing Satan's work in helping to destroy the church by keeping reasonable, educated people on the outside.

Personal Notes

My first university degree was in science and electrical engineering (BSEE). I worked in that capacity for about twenty years, pursuing further education in advanced physics, and earning several patents for my work. Later, I attended a Bible college and seminary, earning a Master of Divinity degree, following which I was ordained as a pastor in a local Baptist church. I served there for some fifteen years. Being rooted in both science and the Bible, I had to endure for years the dilemma of faith in the so-called literal interpretation of creation in the English Bible as well as proven scientific facts. I read many of the statements from the young earth creationists (YECs), knowing all along that some of their conclusions were very wrong. The paradox is obvious. Can I truly be a Christian and not believe in a literal interpretation of the first few chapters of the English Bible? This question haunted me for years.

Some years ago I decided to take matters into my own hands, and with my Bible, a pile of books, a geological toolkit, a large astronomical telescope, and a large RV, I went camping for thirty-one days in the mountains in the American West, primarily in Wyoming, Arizona, and Nevada. It did not take long to discover that I was standing on rocks that contained fossils from the earliest times on earth, layered according to the known geological eras. I spent the whole month visiting archeological digs and dinosaur museums, climbing many hills and giant piles of rocks, collecting fossils and special rocks, reading a dozen or more books on advanced physics and geology in the evenings, and making notes for *And There Was Light*. I began to see the problem. There was a common misunderstanding among the Christian population of the principles of correct biblical hermeneutics (i.e., the principles of interpretation).

The turning point in my understanding of the age of the universe came about when I was reading a science textbook on Maxwell's equations. I was teaching a class on electronic communications systems at a local technical college. I'd been selected to teach this class because of my background in electrical engineering, my experience in radio communication systems, my two licenses from the Federal Communications Commission (FCC), and my college education. I taught for about six years. During this time I felt it necessary to review material about electromagnetic radiation (EMR, or what is sometimes called field theory). I had taken this course in college many years earlier, but as time passed, as many have discovered of themselves, I'd gotten stale in my original studies and the technical jargon and needed a refresher.

So to reestablish my understanding of EMR, I selected a book to read titled *Maxwell on the Electromagnetic Field*, by Thomas K. Simpson.[1] This book was indeed a great refresher in field theory, which I had learned years earlier. However, I discovered one valuable lesson from this study, and that is that the velocity of electromagnetic radiation (i.e., light waves, radio waves, microwaves, gamma rays, and so forth [with electromagnetic radiation referred to as EMR]) was a constant to every observer regardless of the relative velocity of each. Further, I understood the paradox that this velocity (about three hundred million meters per second in free space) is a universal constant that is found in many equations of physics and nuclear theory—and this constant cannot be changed. God had to fix this constant when He created the universe, because this value is incorporated in many of the physical phenomena we accept today. I could spend hours lecturing on the subject, but this is not the purpose of *And There Was Light*. Put simply, the fact of a fixed EMR velocity relative to each observer means that the velocity of light is truly a measure of the age of the universe, and if God ever changed this constant, even the atoms that make up the universe would fall apart. To help in your understanding, the fixed velocity of EMR is part of the mathematics that mandates the electron shell of each atom and is essential to the understanding of quantum physics. Change that and everything falls apart. It can't be changed, because that is the way God created it.

I finally "saw the light" and wrote a title to match: *And There Was Light*. On the cover of this present volume you will find the four basic equations of James Clerk Maxwell. These equations were developed by Maxwell by using the electrical data collected through years of experimentation by Michael Faraday. Both of these men were devoted Christians who understood the basic principle of science: to understand and reveal God's creation to humankind.

Given the overwhelming wealth of proven evidence, I can say with confidence that the universe was created sometime about 13.76 billion years ago and the solar system with the earth was formed later, about 4.5 billion years ago. Further, let me say that God has no reason to fool humankind, and He has stated that He would not. And further still, the Bible gives us no evidence as to when the universe was created. Lastly, this is not the reason God wrote the Bible in the first place. What the YECs fail to understand is simply that the Bible does not give us enough information to date the creation of the universe, nor does the Bible give enough information on God's process and methods in creation. God never intended to give us all this information. If He had, we probably would not understand it anyway. Therefore, let us agree that God created it all, in His time and using His methods. So let it rest, and may we have peace in the church concerning this subject.

May God be glorified forever and forever through Jesus Christ His Son! Amen!

[1] Thomas K. Simpson, *Maxwell on the Electromagnetic Field* (New Brunswick, NJ: Rutgers University Press, 2006).

Bibliography

Africa, Thomas W. *The Ancient World*. Boston: Houghton Mifflin Co., 1969.

Bandstra, Barry. *Genesis 1 - 11, A Handbook on the Hebrew Text*. Waco, Tx: Baylor University Press, 2008.

Bavinck, Herman. *Our Reasonable Faith, A Survey of Christian Doctrine*. Grand Rapids, Mi.: Baker Book House, 1978.

Berkhof, Louis. *Systematic Theology*. Grand Rapids: Eerdmans Publishing, 1974.

Botterweck, G. Johannes, Helmer Ringgren, and Heinz Josef Fabry. *Theological Dictionary of the Old Testament, Vol XIII*. Grand Rapids: Eerdmans Publishing Co., 1992.

Brown, Francis, S. R. Driver, and Charles A. Briggs. *Hebrew and English Lexicon of the Old Testament*. Oxford: Oxford University Press, 1978.

Buswell, J. Oliver. *A Systematic Theology of the Christian Religion*. Grand Rapids: Zondervan, 1977.

Clarke, William N. *An Ouline of Christian Theology*. New York: Charles Scribners Sons, 1916.

Collins, C. John. *Genesis 1 - 4, ALinguistic, Literary, and Theological Commentary*. Phillipsburg, N.J.: P&R Publishing Co., 2006.

Custance, Arther C. *Time and Eternity*. Grand Rapids: Zondervan, 1977.

—. *Without Form and Void*. Brookville, Canada: Custance Publication, 1970.

Dolling, Lisa M, Arther F. Gianelli, and Glenn N. Statile. *The Tests of Time, Readings in the Development of Physical Theory*. Princeton: Princeton University Press, 2003.

Dr. J.H. Hertz, Chief Rabbi. *The Pentateuch and Haftorahs*. London: Oxford University Press, 1940.

Erickson, Millard J. *Christian Theology*. Grand Rapids: Baker Book House, 1985.

Friedman, Richard E. *Commentary on the Torah with English and Hebrew text*. New York: HarperCollins, 2003.

Gleason L. Archer, Jr. *A Survey of the Old Testament Introduction*. Chicago: Moody Press, 1977.

Grudem, Wayne. *Systematic Theology, An Introduction to Biblical Doctrine*. Grand Rapids: Zondervan, 1994.

Gundry, Stanley N., and Roger R. Johnson. *Tensions in Contemporary Theology*. Chicago: Moody Press, 1978.

Hagopian, David G. *The G3N3S1S Debate*. Mission Viejo, Ca.: CruXpress, 2001.

Hawking, Stehen. *A Brief History of Time/ The Universe in a Nutshell*. New York: Bantam Books, 2001.

Henley, Ernest M. *Subatomic Physics*. Hackensack, N.J.: World Scientific Publishing, 2007.

Hodge, Charles. *Systematic Theology*. Grand Rapids: Eerdmans Printing Co., 1979.

Jewish Publication Society. *JPS Hebrew- English Tanakh*. Philadelphia: Jewish Publication Society, 2000.

Kaiser, Walter C. *Toward an Exegetical Theology*. Grand Rapids: Baker Book House, 1981.

Kramer, S. N. *History Begins at Sumer*. London: Thames and Hudson, 1961.

Lennox, John C. *Seven Days that Divide the World*. Grand Rapids: Zondervan, 2011.

Livingston, G. Herbert. *The Pentateuch in its Cultural Environment*. Grand Rapids: Baker Book House, 1974.

Malley, Marjorie C. *Radioactivity, A History of a Mysterious Science*. New York: Oxford University Press, 2011.

McClintock, John, and James Strong. *Cyclopedia of Biblical, Theological, and Ecclesiastical Literature*. Grand Rapids: BakerBook House, 1981.

Mickelsen, A. Berkeley. *Interpereting the Bible*. Grand Rapids, Mich.: Wm. B. Eerdmans, 1977.

Montgomery, David R. *The Rocks Don't Lie*. New York: W.W. Norton & Co., 2012.

Nissen, Hans J. *The Early History of the Ancient Near East, 9000 - 2000 B.C.* Chicago: University of Chicago, 1990.

Packer, James I., Merrill C. Tenney, and William White. *Everyday Life in the Bible, in 2 vol*. New York: Bonanza Books, 1989.

Pfeiffer, Charles F. *The Biblical World*. Nashville: Broadman Press, 1976.

Ramm, Bernard. *The Christian View of Science and Scripture*. Grand Rapids: Eerdmanns Publishing, 1955.

Ross, Hugh. *A Matter of Days*. Colorado Springs: NAVPRESS, 2004.

—. *A Matter of Days*. Canada: NavPress, 2004.

—. *Creation as Science*. Colorado Springs: NAVPRESS Books, 2006.

—. *Navigating Genesis*. Covina, Ca.: RTB Press, 2014.

—. *The Creator and the Cosmos*. Colorado Springs: NAVPRESS, 2001.

—. *The Genesis Question*. Colorado Springs: NAVPRESS, 2001.

Sailamer, John. *Genesis Unbound*. Portland, Or.: Dawson Media, 2011.

Schaeffer, Francis A. *Genesis in Space and Time*. Downers Grove, Ill.: InterVarsity Press, 1975.

—. *No Final Conflict*. Downers Grove, Ill.: InterVarsity Press, 1975.

Shedd, William G.T. *Dogmatic Theology*. Minneapolis: Klock & Klock, 1889, 1979 reprint.

Tenney, Merrill C. *The Zondervan Pictorial Encyclopedia of the Bible*. Grand Rapids: Zondervan, 1975.

Walter C. Kaiser, Jr. *Toward an Exegetical Theology*. Grand Rapids: Baker Book House, 1981.

Walton, John H. *Genesis 1 as Ancient Cosmology*. Winona Lake, In.: Eisenbrauns, Inc., 2011.

—. *The Lost World of Genesis One*. Downers Grove, Ill.: Intervarsity Press, 2009.

Warfield, Benjamin B. *Biblical and Theological Studies*. Philadelphia: Presbyterian & Reformed Publishing Co., 1968.

Weintraub, D. A. *How Old is the Universe?* Princeton, N.J.: Princeton University Press, 2011.

Wenham, Gordon J. *Word Biblical Commentary, Vol. 1*. Waco, Tx.: Word Books, 1987.

Young, Edward J. "Studies in Genesis One." *An International Library of Philosophy and Theology*, 1976: 43 -76.

Whitcomb, John C., Henry M. Morris, *The Genesis Flood*, Grand Rapids, Baker Book House, 1977

Printed in the United States
By Bookmasters